Excel for
Scientists

by

Dr. Gerard M. Verschuuren

Holy Macro Books

Excel for Scientists
Copyright© 2005 by Dr. Gerard M. Verschuuren

Written by:
Dr. Gerard M. Verschuuren

Edited by:
Linda DeLonais

On the Cover:
Design by Shannon Mattiza

Published by:
Holy Macro! Books
13386 Judy Avenue Northwest
Uniontown, Ohio, USA 44685

Distributed by:
Holy Macro! Books

First printing:
August 2005
Printed in the United States of America

Library of Congress Data
Dr. Gerard M. Verschuuren
        Excel for Scientists / Dr. Gerard M. Verschuuren
Library of Congress Control Number: 2005929674

ISBN: 1-932802-10-X

Excel for Scientists

Table of Contents

About the Author

Dr. Gerard M. Verschuuren is a Microsoft Certified Professional specialized in VB, VBA, and VB.NET. He has more than 20 years of experience in teaching at colleges and corporations.

Dr. Verschuuren holds Master's degrees in Biology (Human Genetics) and in Philosophy, plus a Doctorate in the Philosophy of Science from Universities in Europe.

He is the author of Life Scientists, Their Convictions, Their Activities, and Their Values (1995, Genesis Publishing Company).

He is also the author behind the **Visual Learning Series** (MrExcel.com):

- *Slide Your Way Through Excel VBA (2003)*
- *Join the Excellers League (2004)*
- *Your Access to the World (2004)*
- *Master the Web (2005)*
- *Access VBA Made Accessible (2005)*

Prologue

This book can be used on its own or in conjunction with an interactive CD called "Excel for Scientists," also available from the Publisher. This book assumes at least a basic knowledge of Excel. Readers new to Excel may want to familiarize themselves with a basic "how-to" book such as Learn Excel from Mr Excel (ISBN 1-932802-12-6), available from MrExcel.com.

Scientists do not want nor do they need verbose explanations. That's the reason why I tried to be as concise as possible in the chapters of this book. I also attempted to add some meaningful simple exercises, because the proof is still in the pudding.

Since I am a human geneticist myself, most of my simple examples stem from the life sciences. I apologize to all the readers who feel foreign to the cases I use in this book. I hope those readers can look through the surface.

Excel was originally created as a financial application, but it has evolved into a rather sophisticated scientific tool. Although other and perhaps more advanced programs do exist, many of those have a steep learning curve. And that is why Excel still may be your best choice. I hope you will soon discover why.

gmv

Chapter I: General Techniques

There are some general techniques in Excel that every scientist should know about. These techniques will make your work easier and faster, and you will need them in all the chapters to come.

- How do you copy information from your spreadsheets?
- How do you refer to (the contents of) other cells?
- How do you use Names in Excel spreadsheets?
- What is behind your values: Appearance or Reality?
- How do you manipulate dates?
- How do you place functions inside functions?

For a more general coverage of these issues, consult the interactive CD called "*Join the Excellers League*" published by MrExcel. This CD is available through *www.mrexcel.com* or *www.amazon.com*.

Making Copies and Trends

You are probably familiar with the most common copy and paste routines in Excel. Select the cell(s) to copy from, and then choose one of the following options:

1. Hit the Copy button, select a new cell, and hit the Paste button.
2. Choose *Edit / Copy*, select a new cell, and choose Edit/Paste button.
3. Press Ctrl+C, select a new cell, and press Ctrl+V.
4. Right-Click (R-Click) on your selection, choose Copy, R-Click on a new cell, and choose Paste.

But there are also a few other, even fancier ways that we will discuss next.

Using Paste Special

Sometimes, you don't want an exact replica of the copied cells, but a modified version instead. That's when you need the Paste Special option from either the Edit menu or from the R-Click menu.

Say you have some values in your spreadsheet based on a certain formula but you don't want these calculated values to change anymore (see Figure - 1):

1. Select all formula results.
2. Copy these cells.
3. Select *Paste Special* from the *Edit* menu.
4. Choose *Paste ⊙ Values* + hit OK.

Now all your formulas have been replaced with values!

Figure - 1

You can replacing your formulas with values using *Copy / Paste Special / Values.*

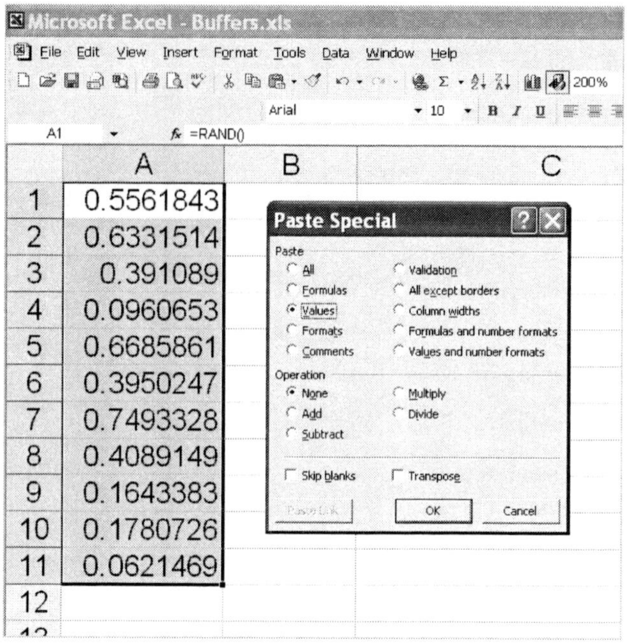

The Paste Special menu has many more powerful options. Let's assume you have replaced formulas with values, but you need to update these static values with a certain factor – say, a multiplication by 1.1:

1. Type your multiplier 1.1 in a cell somewhere on the sheet.
2. Copy that specific cell.
   p.s. Don't forget this step; Excel can't read minds!
3. Select the cells that need to be updated.
4. Choose *Edit / Paste Special.*
5. Select *Operation ⊙ Multiply.*

How can you display all formulas at once? By using Ctrl ~ (the Ctrl key plus the ~ (Tilda) key). This is a toggle option that allows you to switch back and forth between the *value* view and the *formula* view.

Figure - 2

The combination of Ctrl and ~ makes the sheet toggle between value view and formula view.

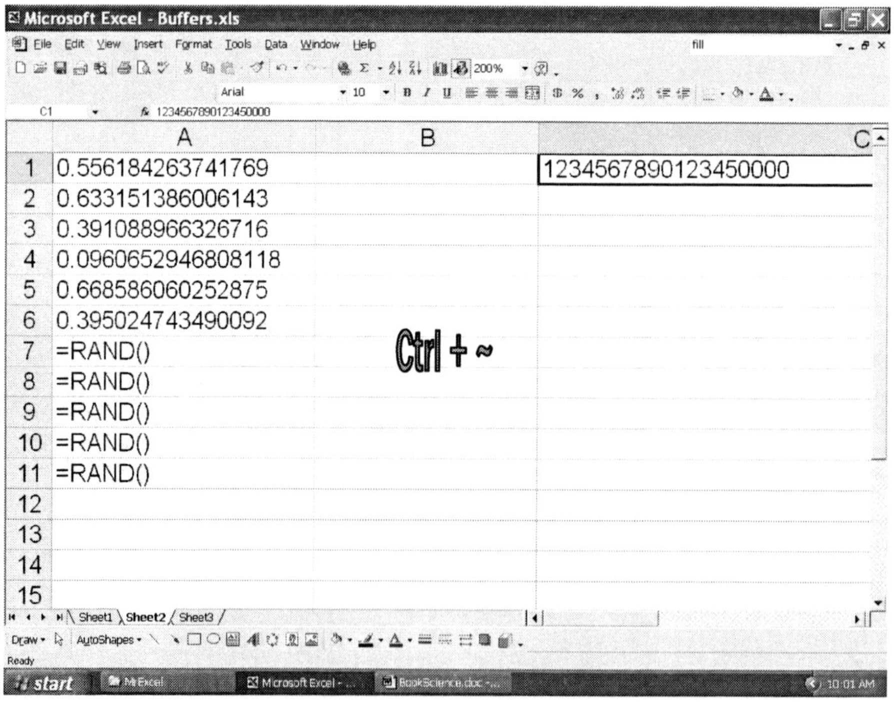

Filling Adjacent Cells

Excel has a special tool, called the *AutoFill Handle*, that allows you to automatically fill adjacent cells. This handle is located in the cell's (or a selection's) right lower corner. When you move the cursor there, it changes into a small plus sign (+):

🧪 You can L-Click and drag this handle down to copy cells

🧪 You can R-Click and drag this handle down to get a menu with options to choose from.

Figure - 3

By dragging the AutoFill handle down with a R-Click, you get a menu with many powerful options, particularly the Series option.

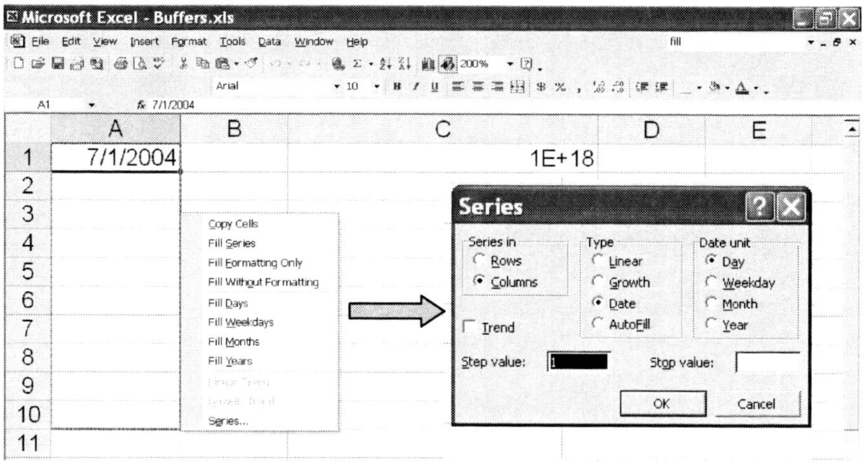

Using a R-Click-drag, you have several options to choose from (especially for dates). *Series*, the last one, is the most powerful because it allows you to specify the step by which you want to increment (see Figure - 3). You can even type "–5" to go five days back, and there is also a choice to skip weekends.

Another way of creating trends is to select two or more cells at the same time and, using the AutoFill Handle with a L-Click drag, to continue the selected pattern.

Excel also has some built in lists (see Table - 1) that the AutoFill handle can use.

Table - 1

Built-in lists supported by Excel

Initial selection	Extended series
1, 2, 3	4, 5, 6
9:00	10:00, 11:00, 12:00
Mon	Tue, Wed, Thu
Monday	Tuesday, Wednesday,
Jan	Feb, Mar, Apr
Jan, Apr	Jul, Oct, Jan
Jan-99, Apr-99	Jul-99, Oct-99, Jan-00
15-Jan, 15-Apr	15-Jul, 15-Oct
1999, 2000	2001, 2002, 2003
1-Jan, 1-Mar	1-May, 1-Jul, 1-Sep,...
Qtr3 (or Q3 or Quarter3)	Qtr4, Qtr1, Qtr2,...

Initial selection	Extended series
text1, textA	text2, textA, text3, textA,...
first Period	second Period, 3rd Period,...
Product 1	Product 2, Product 3,...

To add your own customized list(s), do the following:

1. Select *Tools / Options / Custom Lists*.
2. Type your entries, clicking Add after each one (see Figure - 4).

Figure - 4

The *Tools/Options/Custom Lists* dialog box lets you add your own customized list of entries.

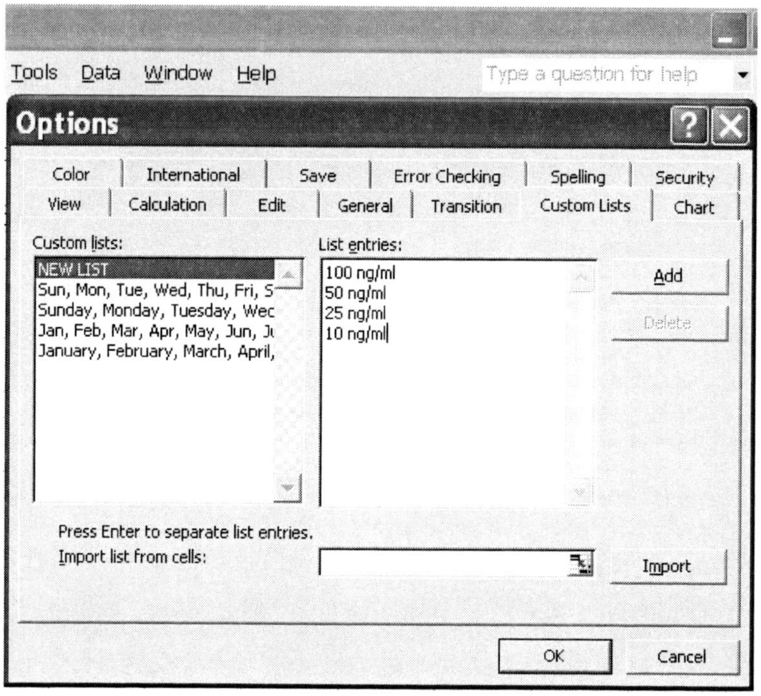

Navigating Quickly

Let's say that you want the same formula in the cells A1:A200. What is the most efficient way of doing such a thing?

1. Select cell A1.
2. Select *Edit / GoTo / Reference: A200*.
3. Do NOT hit Enter by itself; instead, hit Shift + Enter (or Shift + OK). The Shift key will also select the cells in between A1 and A200, even though you are actually still in cell A1 (white) (unless you click somewhere else, so don't do this!).
4. In the formula bar, type: =RAND()
5. Do not hit Enter, for that would take you to A2 (and you would have to type the formula again). Instead, you want this formula to be in all the selected cells, so hit Ctrl + Enter. The Ctrl key inserts the formula in <u>all</u> selected cells

Let's say that you want cell B1 to display the sum of A1:A200. When you select cell B1 plus the *AutoSum* button (Σ),you see only: =SUM(). How can you get the total range in there?

1. Click in A1. Now you see: =SUM(A1)
2. Hold both Shift + Ctrl and press the Down-Arrow key (↓). Voila!

Table - 2	Combination	Effect
Important combinations with the Enter key	Shift + Enter	Selects all cells in between the two selected cells
	Ctrl + Enter	Copies a formula/value into all selected cells
	Ctrl + Shift + Enter	Creates an array formula in all selected cells (see Array Formulas on page 75)
	Ctrl + Shift + ⇩	Selects all cells up to next empty cell

Understanding Relative versus Absolute

When you copy a formula in any direction, cell references such as "A1" will change accordingly because they are actually *relative* cell references – something like "one cell up" or "one cell to the left."

To make all or part of a cell reference absolute, you need to apply the "$" sign to the row and/or column symbol. This can be done easily by hitting the *F4* key (after selecting or typing a specific cell address).

The F4 key is actually a cycle key: it goes from A1 to $A$1 to A$1 to $A1 and back to A1. When you copy formulas like these, they will behave as shown in Figure - 5:

Figure - 5

Using the F4 key for a cell address like A1 cycles through four different settings: $A$1, A$1, $A1, A1. The differences between these settings show up when you try to copy the formula to neighboring cells.

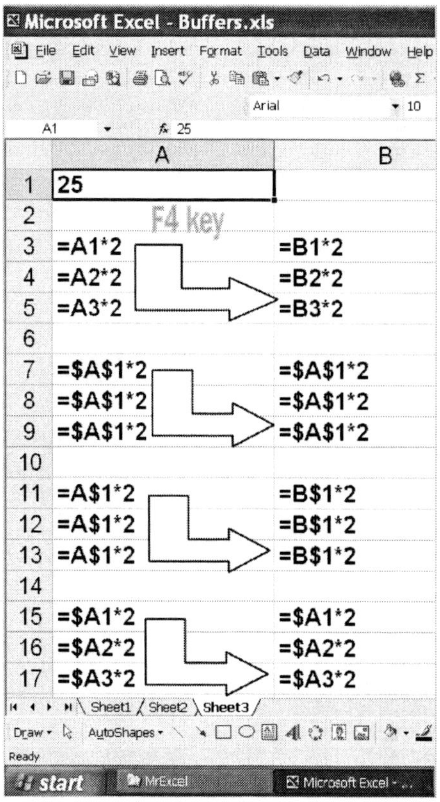

Naming Cells

Another way of creating *absolute* cell addresses is to give one or more cells a specific name. This name can then be used in formulas as an absolute cell reference:

1. Select the cell(s) you want to name.
2. Click inside the Name box (the first box on the formula bar).
3. Type a (unique) name – either without spaces or using underscores in place of spaces (e.g., My_Name).
4. Hit Enter.
5. The dropdown list of the Name box now holds the new name, which is accessible from any sheet in your book.

If you ever need to change or delete the address "behind" a name, go to *Insert / Name / Define* (see Figure - 6).

⚗ To change: Select the name and change the reference at the bottom

⚗ To delete: Select the name and hit the Delete button

From now on, you can use this name in formulas. This is one way to make your formulas more "readable."

Names are also great when you want to refer to a list of items or a table of values in formulas. Later on, we will see that many functions need to know the range of cells in which to search. Supply them with a name!

Another nice feature of names is that they refer not only to cell addresses but also to specific values. Say you often need to use a certain constant in your formulas:

1. Go to *Insert / Name / Define*.
2. Type the name of the constant, such as "signif".
3. In *Reference*: type the constant's value preceded by an equal sign, e.g. =0.975.

You can now use the "=A1*signif" name in formulas. Plus, whenever you change the constant behind the name, all formulas using it will automatically update!

Figure - 6

Names can also refer to constants. When using names for constants in formulas, the formula results change whenever the reference changes.

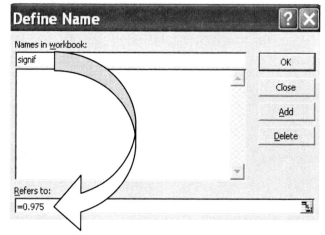

Names function at the <u>book</u> level, which means that you can access them from anywhere in the book, on any sheet. However, if you want to create a sheet-level name, you must add the sheet's name followed by an exclamation mark:

Sheet1!MyCell

Names can even be dynamic, provided you use the OFFSET function to define them under *Insert / Name / Define.*

=OFFSET(Start, 0, 0, Rows, Cols)

Figure - 7

COUNTA(A:A) will count all cells in column A that contain entries (numbers or not).

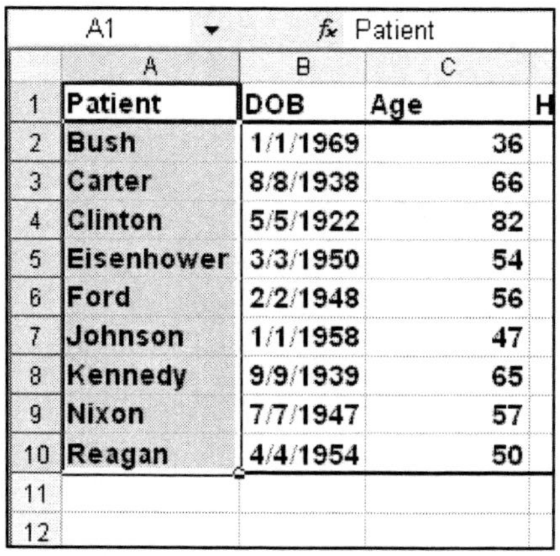

	A	B	C	
	A1 ▾	*fx* Patient		
1	Patient	DOB	Age	H
2	Bush	1/1/1969	36	
3	Carter	8/8/1938	66	
4	Clinton	5/5/1922	82	
5	Eisenhower	3/3/1950	54	
6	Ford	2/2/1948	56	
7	Johnson	1/1/1958	47	
8	Kennedy	9/9/1939	65	
9	Nixon	7/7/1947	57	
10	Reagan	4/4/1954	50	
11				
12				

The range A1:A10 in Figure - 7 has been given a name – in this case, "Patient". You may have to change this reference if you add new patients at the bottom. Instead, you could count how many cells in column *A* have something in them (number or not) by using:

COUNTA(A:A)

This count can then be used in the Patient reference, provided you make sure there are no hidden figures farther down in column A:

=OFFSET(A1, 0, 0, COUNTA(A:A))

 Note:

Unlike COUNTA, COUNT will only count cells that have numbers in them.

From now on, the name "Patient" can be used in any formula and it will include all future additions (see Figure - 8).

Figure - 8

Names can refer not only to a static range, but also to a dynamic range of cells by using the OFFSET function.

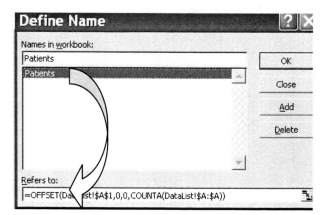

Telling Appearance from Reality

Numbers in Excel are stored with a maximum precision of 15 digits and/or decimals. You can change the "look" of a number by using *formatting* tools – such as Format/Cells or the Currency Style, Percent Style, and Increase/Decrease Decimal buttons (see Figure - 9).

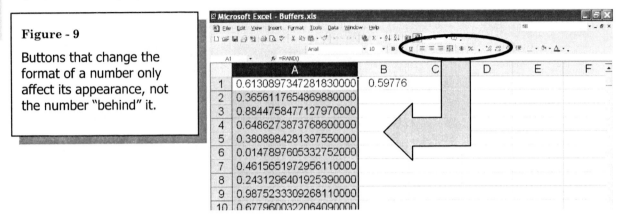

Figure - 9

Buttons that change the format of a number only affect its appearance, not the number "behind" it.

However, changing the look of a number does not change the real number in the background. Excel will still use the entire number (up to 15 digits and or decimals) in its calculations. What are the consequences?

➢ A number like 123,456,789,123,456,789 will show up as 123456789123456**000**

➢ A number like 0.123456789123456789 will show up as 0.123456789123456

With Format/Cells/Number, you can also choose a scientific notation – which again is a matter of "looks." This way, 0.123456789123456 would be shown as 1.2346E-01 if you decide to display four decimals.

To really change a number, you need functions such as INT(), ROUND(), ROUNDUP(), or ROUNDDOWN().With the function ROUND(X, n), for instance, you can also specify a number's (X's) number of decimals (n). Table - 3 gives you an overview of some useful rounding functions.

Table - 3

Different rounding functions

Down ⇦   ⇨ Up
-3 -2 -1 0 1 2 3

Function	Effect
INT(...)	Down to the nearest integer
TRUNC(..., 0)	Removes fractional part (0 for fully; other numbers remove to specified number of decimal places)
EVEN(...)	Up to the nearest even integer
ODD(...)	Up to the nearest odd integer
FLOOR(..., 0.5)	Down (toward zero) in multiples of 0.5
CEIL(..., 0.5)	Up (away from zero) in multiples of 0.5
ROUND(..., 0)	Up or down to nearest integer
ROUNDUP(..., 0)	Up to nearest integer (away from zero)
ROUNDDOWN(..., 0)	Down to nearest integer (toward zero)

Table - 4

This chart shows you how rounding functions actually behave.

	4.95446271	5.24145729	8.46530939	9.91674185	4.43501107	-8.35694403	-5.66060902
ABS	4.95446271	5.24145729	8.46530939	9.91674185	4.43501107	8.356944032	5.660609021
INT	4	5	8	9	4	-9	-6
TRUNC	4	5	8	9	4	-8	-5
FLOOR(..., 0.5)	4.5	5	8	9.5	4	#NUM!	#NUM!
FLOOR(..., -0.5)	#NUM!	#NUM!	#NUM!	#NUM!	#NUM!	-8	-5.5
CEIL(..., 0.5)	5	5.5	8.5	10	4.5	#NUM!	#NUM!
CEIL(..., -0.5)	#NUM!	#NUM!	#NUM!	#NUM!	#NUM!	-8.5	-6
EVEN	6	6	10	10	6	-10	-6
ODD	5	7	9	11	5	-9	-7
ROUND(..., 2)	4.95	5.24	8.47	9.92	4.44	-8.36	-5.66
ROUNDDOWN	4.95	5.24	8.46	9.91	4.43	-8.35	-5.66
ROUNDUP	4.96	5.25	8.47	9.92	4.44	-8.36	-5.67
ROUNDEVEN	-	-	-	-	-	-	-

Managing Dates

Dates in Excel are also not the way they appear. When you see 1/1/1900, Excel actually stores the serial number 1. The number "2" represents "Jan 2 1900" – and today's number could be something like "38500". What's the purpose of all of this? The reason is quite simple: You can calculate with dates, adding and subtracting them like numbers!

In addition, each serial number allows for decimals as part of a day. A number like 1.5 stands for 1/1/1900 12:00 p.m. Time is expressed as a decimal based on 24 hours.

The issue of how you want to display this number is a matter of formatting:

> m/d/yy: 1/1/00
> mm/dd/yyyy: 01/01/1900
> dddd mmm-d: Monday Jan-1
> m/d/yy h:mm:ss: 1/1/00 12:00:00

There are also some great date functions:

> =TODAY():   e.g., 38500
> =NOW():   e.g., 38500.1234567890
> =NOW()–TODAY(): e.g., 0.123456789

Given this information, we should be able to work with dates more comfortably.

We can add, subtract, sum, and average time information – as long as we use the format *h:mm:ss.*

When date and time are involved, the difference between two values may be more than 24 hours. This requires a special format: [h]:mm:ss.

If you prefer to deal with time as a decimal of hours – e.g. 8.5 instead of 8:30 – then you need to convert this time information into day decimals: Just divide by 24 (hours). If the total goes beyond 24 hours, you have to use the format [h]:mm:ss again (see Figure - 10).

Figure - 10

Working with regular time settings and decimal time settings

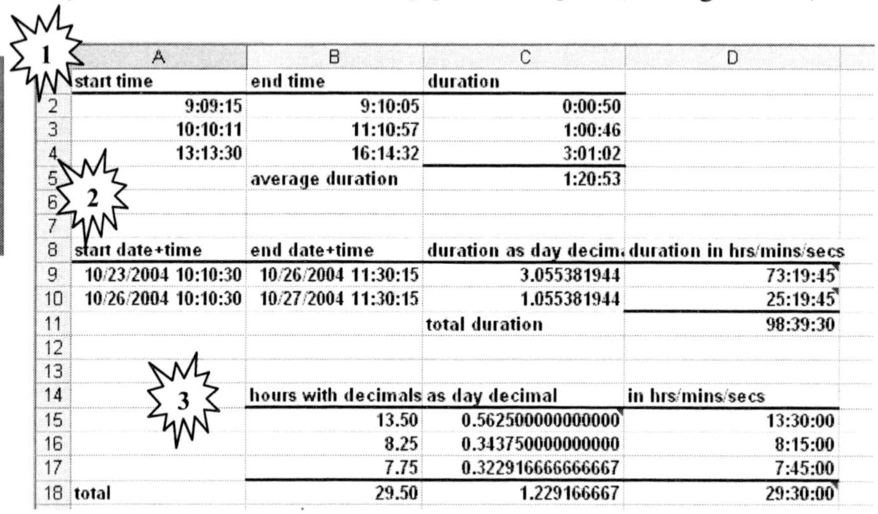

	A	B	C	D
1	start time	end time	duration	
2	9:09:15	9:10:05	0:00:50	
3	10:10:11	11:10:57	1:00:46	
4	13:13:30	16:14:32	3:01:02	
5		average duration	1:20:53	
6				
7				
8	start date+time	end date+time	duration as day decim	duration in hrs/mins/secs
9	10/23/2004 10:10:30	10/26/2004 11:30:15	3.055381944	73:19:45
10	10/26/2004 10:10:30	10/27/2004 11:30:15	1.055381944	25:19:45
11			total duration	98:39:30
12				
13				
14		hours with decimals	as day decimal	in hrs/mins/secs
15		13.50	0.562500000000000	13:30:00
16		8.25	0.343750000000000	8:15:00
17		7.75	0.322916666666667	7:45:00
18	total	29.50	1.229166667	29:30:00

Putting Functions Inside Functions

All formulas in Excel are based on calculations and/or functions (see Table - 6):

◔ *Calculations* work with operators such as (), ^, *, /, +, and –. These operators work in a certain order of precedence, so 2+4/2 is 4 in Excel, whereas (2+4)/2 returns 3.

Table - 5

Excel performs math operations in a specific order

Operator	()	^	*	/	+	–
Precedence	1	2	3		4	

◔ *Functions* are built in operations, such as =SUM(A1:A3), which is equivalent to the calculation =A1+A2+A3. Most functions accept or require one or more *arguments* inside their parentheses.

◔ Formulas can also be a combination of calculations and functions – for instance, =SUM(A1:A3)*0.05, or =NOW()+30.

◔ Formulas can also "nest" functions inside functions – such as: =ROUND(SUM(A1:A3), 2).

Formulas	
Calculations	Functions
( ) ^ * / + -	SUM(), COUNT(), IF(), …
Nested calculations	Nested functions
((A1+A2)*(B1+B2))/C1	ROUND(SUM(A1:A3), 2)
Calculations plus functions	
0.05 * SUM(A1:A3)	

Table - 6

Formulas always start with an equal sign. They are based on calculations and/or functions.

The question is: How do you type a function that has a complex syntax behind it? If you know its syntax and the order of arguments, you can just type the function (from Excel 2002 on, you even get help while you are typing the function).

But what if you don't know the syntax yet? There are several options on the toolbar (depending on your Excel version):

- You can use the f_x button (either on the toolbar or on the formula bar).

- There may also be a drop-down button next to the Σ button (AutoSum) on the toolbar.

 Note:

The Σ button covers one function; the f_x button covers them all.

Through these options, you get a complete listing of all the functions available in Excel. Select the function you want and use the new dialog box to provide the arguments that the function calls for.

What to do if one of the function's arguments requires a new (nested) function? Do not use the f_x button again, but instead click on the formula bar's first button (in this case SUM; see left-most arrow in Figure - 11). This opens a new dialog box, although the total formula remains visible in the formula bar.

Figure - 11

The SUM function is "nested" within the ROUND function. You can switch back and forth between both functions by clicking on each function's name in the formula bar.

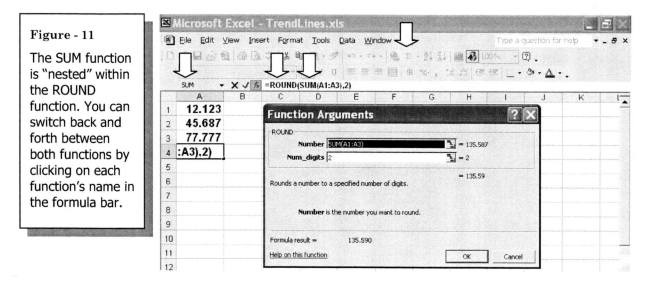

Provide the information for the second function. If you are completely done, hit OK. If you need to go back to the first function, click on its name in the formula bar. This opens the first dialog box once again.

The exercises that follow are intended to reinforce the information just presented. You will find similar exercises throughout the remainder of this book. The answers to questions posed in these exercises can be found in the Answers to Exercises section on page 104.

Exercise 1.

1. Start with a new spreadsheet and type the following labels:
   a. In A1: [AH]
   b. In B1: [A$^-$]
   c. In C1: K_a = 4.7
2. In column A, put in the percentages of acetic acid [AH]. They go from 98, 96, 94, and so forth down to 2. Fill the column the easiest and fastest way possible.
3. In column B, put a calculation for the percentage of acetate [A$^-$]:
   a. Select B2 through B50 (Hint: Use Go To + Shift).
   b. Type your formula: =100–A2
   c. Enter this formula in all cells.
4. In column C, calculate the pH of the solution:
   a. Select C2 through C50.
   b. Use this formula: =C1 + LOG10(B2/A2)
   c. Make sure you have the right type of reference for C1: $C$1
   d. Enter this formula in all cells.
5. Save the table.

Exercise 2.

1. Start with a new spreadsheet and use the information from Figure - 12.
2. Calculate the time lapse.
3. Format the cells properly.
4. Calculate glucose mol/min.

Figure - 12

Measuring changes in glucose levels after certain time intervals.

	A	B	C	D	E
1			Lactose added to identical cultures of bacteria		
2					
3	Start	End	Time lapse	glucose mol/l	glucose mol/min
4	9:55:00	10:25:00		26	
5	10:00:00	11:00:00		38	
6	10:05:00	11:35:00		48	
7	10:10:00	12:10:00		57	

Chapter II: Statistical Analysis

Understanding Sampling Distributions

Measurements are usually based on a *sample* taken from the total *population* (see Figure - 13).

This sample can be either:

> ➤ a test group taken from the total population or
> ➤ a finite series of measurements done from among an infinite number of potential measurements.

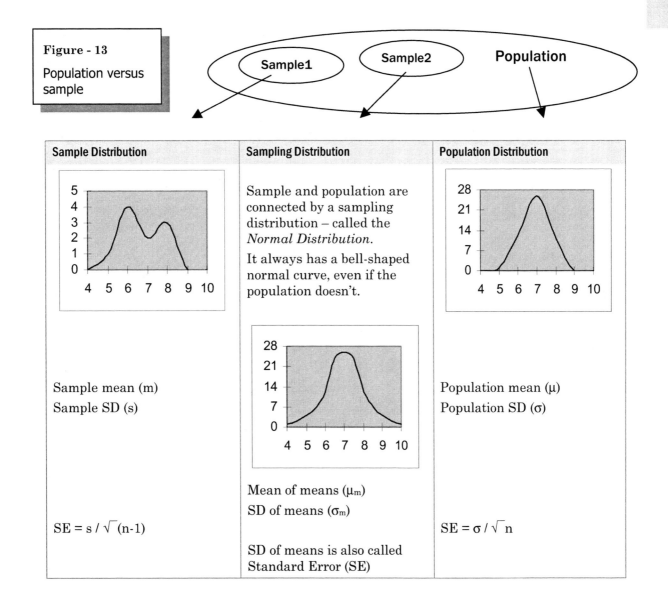

Figure - 13

Population versus sample

Sample Distribution	Sampling Distribution	Population Distribution
	Sample and population are connected by a sampling distribution – called the *Normal Distribution*. It always has a bell-shaped normal curve, even if the population doesn't.	
Sample mean (m) Sample SD (s)	Mean of means (μ_m) SD of means (σ_m)	Population mean (μ) Population SD (σ)
$SE = s / \sqrt{(n-1)}$	SD of means is also called Standard Error (SE)	$SE = \sigma / \sqrt{n}$

Using Normal Distribution

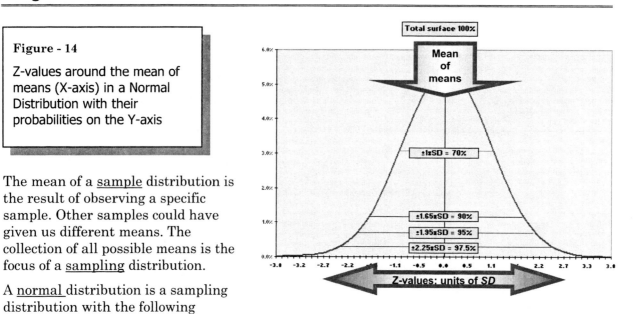

Figure - 14

Z-values around the mean of means (X-axis) in a Normal Distribution with their probabilities on the Y-axis

II

The mean of a <u>sample</u> distribution is the result of observing a specific sample. Other samples could have given us different means. The collection of all possible means is the focus of a <u>sampling</u> distribution.

A <u>normal</u> distribution is a sampling distribution with the following properties:

- 1x the StDev around the mean is 70% of its total surface (= 1 x SE)

- 1.65x StDev is 90% (= 1.65 x SE)

The Z-value is plotted on the X-axis of Figure - 14. The Z-value represents the distance between a specific mean and "the *Mean* of the means," expressed in units of *Standard Error* (which is the *Standard Deviation* of the means).

Table - 7 Excel functions used to find specific statistical values

Description	Function
Mean of a range of numbers	=AVERAGE(*range*)
Standard deviation of a range of numbers	=STDEV(*range*)
Skewness of a range of numbers: skewed far to the left (–1) or to the right (+1)	=SKEW(*range*)
Kurtosis of a range of numbers (–1 flattened; +1 peaked)	=KURT(*range*)
Z-value of a *number* X in a range of numbers	=STANDARDIZE(X, *mean*, *stdev*)
Distribution's surface to the left of a number X in a range of numbers with a given *mean* and *stdev* (True makes it cumulative)	=NORMDIST(X, *mean*, *stdev*, *true*)
Cumulative probability (surface) to the left of a Z-value	=NORMSDIST(Z)
Critical Z-value of a certain *probability* (the Z-value found in a statistics table)	=NORMSINV(*probability*)
Standard deviation of the *means* (SE)	=STDEV(*range*) / SQRT(*n*)

Figure - 15

The Normal and Cumulative Distributions for 100 random numbers, generated with a mean of 10 and a standard deviation of 0.5

	A	B	C	D	E	F	G	H	I	J	K	L
1	9.85		Mean	9.98		skewness						
2	9.36		StDev	0.54		kurtosis						
3	10.12											
4	10.64		X	Frequency	NormDist	From Total	Z	NormsDist				
5	10.6											
6	10.87		8.50	0	0.00	0.32	-2.72	0%				
7	8.91		8.75	1	0.01	0.86	-2.26	1%				
8	9.88		9.00	2	0.04	2.38	-1.80	4%				
9	10.55		9.25	7	0.09	5.39	-1.34	9%				
10	9.46		9.50	9	0.19	9.90	-0.88	19%				
11	9.65		9.75	16	0.34	14.76	-0.42	34%				
12	9.15		10.00	19	0.51	17.87	0.04	51%				
13	9.08		10.25	13	0.69	17.57	0.50	69%				
14	9.51		10.50	16	0.83	14.03	0.96	83%				
15	9.61		10.75	9	0.92	9.10	1.42	92%				
16	8.94		11.00	5	0.97	4.79	1.88	97%				
17	9.72		11.25	3	0.99	2.05	2.34	99%				
18	9.8		11.50	0	1.00	0.71	2.80	100%				
19	10.07			100								
20	9.82											
21	9.84											

These are some of the formulas used in the spreadsheet shown in Figure - 15:

➢ D1: =AVERAGE(A:A)

➢ D2: =STDEV(A:A)

➢ D6:D18: =FREQUENCY(A:A,C6:C18)
  (array function; see Multiple-cell arrays on page 74.)

➢ E6: =NORMDIST(C6,$D$1, $D$2,TRUE)

➢ F18: =Total*(E18–E17) (and then copied upwards)

➢ G6 holds one of these three options:
  1. =(C6-$D$1)/ $D$2 or
  2. =NORMSINV(E6) or
  3. =STANDARDIZE(C6,$D$1,$D$2)

➢ H6: =NORMSDIST(G6)

Figure - 16

The surface under a bell-shaped curve is based on the difference between the low- and high-end probabilities.

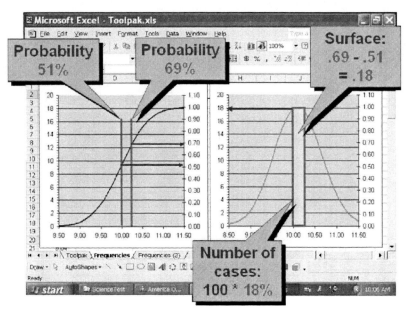

A *Normal Distribution* can be plotted either as cumulative or as non-cumulative. The surface under the bell-shaped curve (right) is 100%, The cumulative curve (left) goes up to 100%.

To calculate the surface of a specific section of a bell-shaped curve (say, the category between 10 and 10.25), subtract the probability (51%) of the bottom value (10) from the probability (69%) of the top value (10.25), and you will find a surface of 18%. So 18% of all cases fits in this category (see Figure - 16).

A *sample* distribution is a frequency distribution of <u>values</u>, whereas a *sampling* distribution is a frequency distribution of <u>means</u>. The mean of a sample distribution is one of the means in a sampling distribution. The ideal sampling distribution is a Normal Distribution. Figure - 17 shows the relationship between both distributions.

II

Figure - 17

The difference between a sample distribution and a sampling distribution using "samples" of ten random numbers between 0 and 10

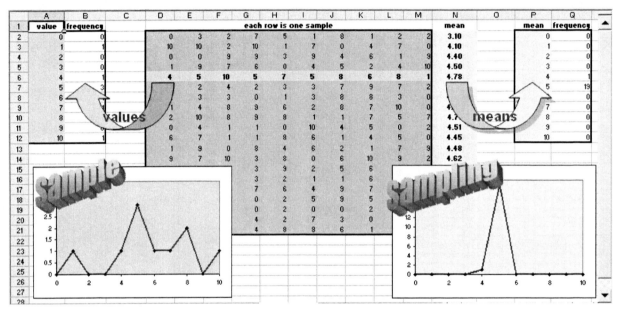

Exercise 3.

1. Fill A1:A10 with these values: 24, 27, 20, 23, 25, 25, 24, 22, 26, 29

2. Find the Mean and StDev.

3. Create these bins: 21, 23, 25, 27, 29

4. Put the frequency next to each bin.

5. Put the Z-value that comes with that bin value next to each bin.

6. Place the cumulative surface area of each Z-value next to that Z-value.

7. Save your file.

Exercise 4.

1. Create a column with 13 Z-values: -3.0, -2.5, ... 2.5, and 3.0

2. Create a second column with the corresponding cumulative surface areas by using the correct function.

3. Save your file.

Using the Random Number Generator

II

The *Random Number Generator* is available through the *Analysis ToolPak*.

To install the Analysis ToolPak, select:

1. Tools
2. Add-Ins
3. Analysis ToolPak

To use the Analysis ToolPak, select:

1. Tools
2. Data Analysis
3. RN Generator.

It may be useful to use the Random Number Generator as provided by the Analysis Toolpak. Implement the following settings:

1. Select one variable (usually, you only need one).
2. Set how many numbers you want to generate – e.g., 100.
3. Determine which mean and standard deviation to use.
4. Take your pick whether you want to create a Normal Distribution or a different kind of distribution (see Figure - 19 for a complete list).
5. If you don't specify a seed, you will always get the same ##.
6. Locate the top cell of your output range.

You can find some basic statistics for the numbers you have generated by using the ToolPak: *Descriptive Statistics*. The results are snapshots and do NOT update (see Figure - 18). In general, therefore, you want to use functions instead of the ToolPak results!

Figure - 18

The Analysis Toolpak provides a static listing of descriptive statistics for a range of values.

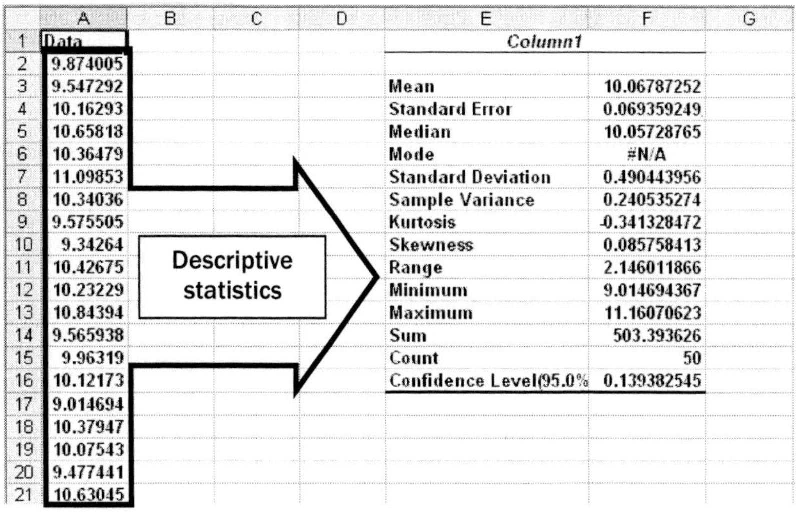

The Random Number Generator can create several kinds of distributions. In Figure - 19, we created 100 random numbers according to each type of distribution available in the Generator.

	A	B	C	D	E	F	G
1	Data					Column1	
2	9.874005						
3	9.547292				Mean	10.06787252	
4	10.16293				Standard Error	0.069359249	
5	10.65818				Median	10.05728765	
6	10.36479				Mode	#N/A	
7	11.09853				Standard Deviation	0.490443956	
8	10.34036				Sample Variance	0.240535274	
9	9.575505				Kurtosis	-0.341328472	
10	9.34264				Skewness	0.085758413	
11	10.42675	Descriptive			Range	2.146011866	
12	10.23229	statistics			Minimum	9.014694367	
13	10.84394				Maximum	11.16070623	
14	9.565938				Sum	503.393626	
15	9.96319				Count	50	
16	10.12173				Confidence Level(95.0%	0.139382545	
17	9.014694						
18	10.37947						
19	10.07543						
20	9.477441						
21	10.63045						

We then calculated a frequency distribution table based on the results produced by the FREQUENCY function (see page 74). Finally, we plotted this frequency distribution in a graph.

Figure - 19 Overview of the kinds of distributions the Random Number Generator can cover

---

Uniform: 100 ## between 0 and 10

Characterized by lower and upper bounds. Variables are drawn with equal probability from all values in the range. A common application uses a uniform distribution in the range 0...1.

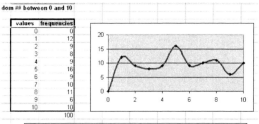

Normal: 100 ## with m=10 and s=0.5

Characterized by a mean and a standard deviation. A common application uses a mean of 0 and a standard deviation of 1 for the standard normal distribution.

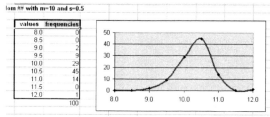

Bernouilli: 100 ## with p=0.5

Characterized by a probability of success (p value) on a given trial. Bernoulli random variables have the value 0 or 1. For example, you can draw a uniform random variable in the range 0...1. If the variable is less than or equal to the probability of success, the Bernoulli random variable is assigned the value 1; otherwise, it is assigned the value 0.

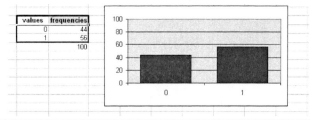

Binomial: 100 ## with p=0.5 and 10 trials

Characterized by a probability of success (*p* value) for a number of trials.

For example, you can generate number-of-trials Bernoulli random variables, the sum of which is a binomial random variable.

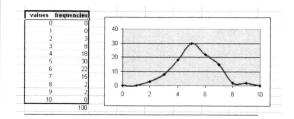

Poisson: 100 ## with lambda=0.5 (=1/mean)

Characterized by a value lambda, equal to 1/mean. Poisson distribution is often used to characterize the number of events that occur per unit of time — for example, the average rate at which cars arrive at a toll plaza.

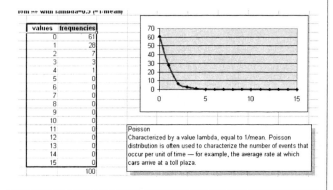

Discrete: 100 ## for the values in the list according to their probabilities

Characterized by a value and the associated probability range. The range must contain two columns: The left column contains values, and the right column contains probabilities associated with the value in that row.

The sum of the probabilities must be 1.

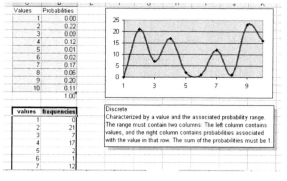

Exercise 5.

1. Use the Random Number Generator for one variable.

2. Create 100 numbers with a mean of 25 and a standard deviation of 0.5 according to a Normal distribution.

3. Display the Descriptive Statistics for those 100 numbers.

4. Also use the AVERAGE, STDEV, KURT, and SKEW functions.

5. Notice the changes that take place when you change one of the random numbers.

6. Try to recreate the formulas used in Figure - 15 on page 15.

Using Student's t-Distribution

The normal probability table used in statistics gives you the sampling distribution for samples of 30 or more.

When working with samples of 30 or less, you must use the *Student's t-distribution*. This is a sampling distribution similar to the normal distribution but with a flatter and wider shape, depending on the sample's size. It works with positive t-scores (+) instead of Z-scores (– and +), and they depend on the sample's size (expressed in *degrees of freedom*). A condition for using the t-Test, however, is the assumption that the population has a normal distribution.

Table - 8

The Excel functions needed to find specific values related to the Student's t-Distribution

Objective	Function
To find the critical t-value for a specific probability and degrees of freedom (table value; always two-tailed; 10% two-tailed is 5% one-tailed)	=TINV(Probability, df)
To find the probability that comes with a specific t-value, two-tailed	=TDIST(t-value,df,2)
To determine the degrees of freedom for n cases	=n–1

Figure - 20

The probabilities of t-values for five different sample sizes (degrees of freedom)

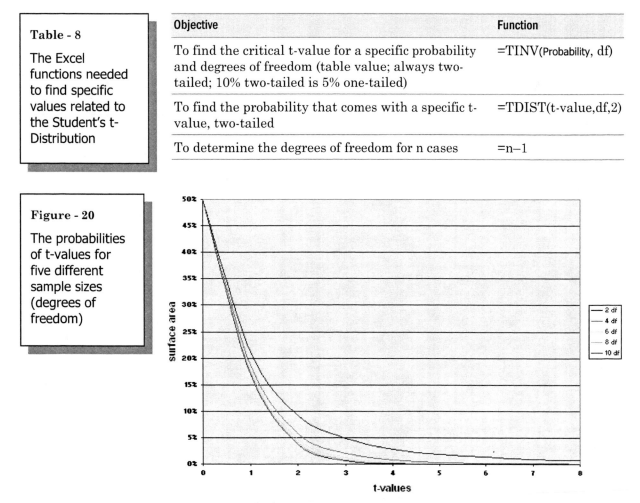

Exercise 6.

1. What are the degrees of freedom in a sample of 25 cases?

2. What is the critical t-value in this sample for a 5% probability?

3. What is the probability that comes with a t-value of 2.06?

4. What is the probability if we want a one-tailed version?

Exercise 7.

1. Create a column with 11 one-tailed t-values: 0, 1, ... 9, and 10

2. Add five columns for different degrees of freedom: 2, 4, 6, 8, and 10

3. Which function do you need to calculate the probabilities?

4. Use one formula for all intersections.

Using Binomial Distribution

Often, populations can be divided into two groups on the basis of some splitting characteristic: male/female, immunized/non-immunized, defect/correct, etc. These are called dichotomous populations.

That's where proportions (p) come in: what is the proportion of "success" or "yes" cases in relationship to all cases. This time we are dealing with a *binomial distribution* (cf. a *Bernouilli* distribution),)which is a cumulative distribution dependant on the proportion (p) of "yes" cases.

Table - 9 The Excel functions needed when working with Binomial Distributions	Binomial Distributions for yes/no proportions.	p = "yes" cases / total cases
	To find the probability of exactly X successes in Y trials given a certain p (for up to X successes: last argument is true)	=BINOMDIST(X, Y, p, false)
	To determine the critical binomial value in n trials for a specific probability given a certain p (the function is always cumulative)	=CRITBINOM(n, probability, p)

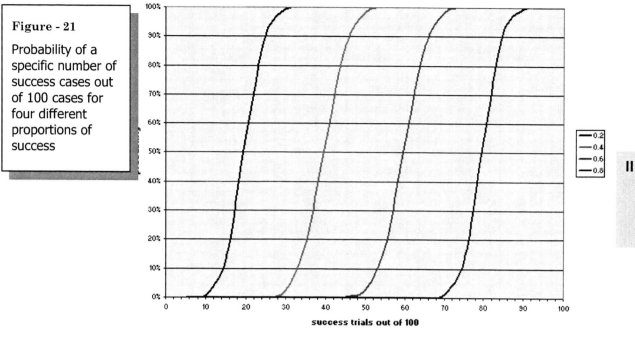

Figure - 21

Probability of a specific number of success cases out of 100 cases for four different proportions of success

---

Exercise 8.

1. What is the exact chance for seven tails in tossing a coin 10x?

2. What is the critical value of tails in tossing a coin 10x at a probability level (alpha) of 12%?

Using Chi-Square Distribution

Instead of analyzing individual cases, as we have done so far, we may want to count cases in specified categories. This is where frequencies come in.

A good sampling distribution for this purpose is the *Chi Square Distribution* (χ^2-Test). The Chi-Square Distribution is not symmetrical, so its value can never be negative. The critical region exists of large positive values of χ^2. Chi-values depend on the number of categories, expressed in *degrees of freedom*.

The Chi-Square Distribution is for frequencies: $\chi^2 = \sum \left[\dfrac{(f_{obs} - f_{exp})^2}{f_{exp}} \right]$

	Objective	Function
Table - 10 The Excel functions for dealing with Chi-Square Distributions	To find the critical Chi-value for a certain probability and n degrees of freedom	=CHIINV(probability, n)
	To find the probability for range X of observed frequencies and range Y of expected frequencies	=CHITEST(X, Y)
	To find the probability for Chi-value χ and n degrees of freedom	=CHIDIST(χ, n)
	To determine the degrees of freedom for X cols and Y rows	=(X–1)*(Y–1)

II

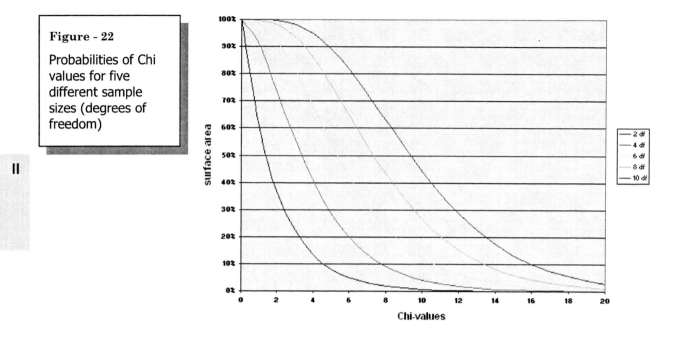

Figure - 22

Probabilities of Chi values for five different sample sizes (degrees of freedom)

 Exercise 9.

1. Create two different frequency tables in A1:B2 and D1:E2 using this data:
   a. Observed: 20 (A1); 15 (B1); 37 (A2); 12 (B2)
   b. Expected: 24 (D1); 11 (E1); 33 (D2); 16 (E2)

2. How many degrees of freedom are there?

3. What is the probability for these two ranges?

4. What is the actual Chi-value for that probability?

5. What is the critical Chi-value at a 5% probability level?

6. What is the probability for the actual Chi-value we have found?

Exercise 10.

1. Create a column with 21 Chi-values from 0 to 20.

2. Add five more columns for different degrees of freedom: 2, 4, 6, 8, and 10

3. At the intersections, calculate the probabilities with CHIDIST.

Estimating with Confidence

Often times, we need to estimate the characteristics of a *population* on the basis of information about a *sample*. For instance, we use the sample's mean to estimate the population's mean.

The amount of confidence we can put in an estimate varies. To deal with this problem,

> ➢ we set a confidence level (usually 95%) and

> ➢ we determine a confidence limit (around the mean).

Look at the example shown in Table - 11. Based on a sample's mean of 44 (and a standard error of 6), we have 95% confidence that the population's mean is between 32 and 56. Consequently, we take a 5% risk (α) of being wrong!

Table - 11									
Example of Z-values and probabilities for specific means, given a mean of means of 44 and a standard error of 6	-3	-2	-1	0	1	2	3	**Z-value**	
	0%	2%	16%	50%	84%	98%	100%	**probability**	
								mean	**stdev**
	26	32	38	44	50	56	62	**44**	**6**

-DIST functions find the probabilities (for a certain distance)

-INV functions find the distances (for a certain probability)

If we were to plot "cumulative" means for one up to 20 samples of 10 values taken from a population of random numbers between 0 and 10 (see Figure - 23), the mean would fluctuate. Yet, the mean would gradually stabilize at the population's mean (which is 5).

Figure - 23

By increasing the sample size (in this example: from 10 to 20 ... to 200), the mean gradually stabilizes at the population's mean.

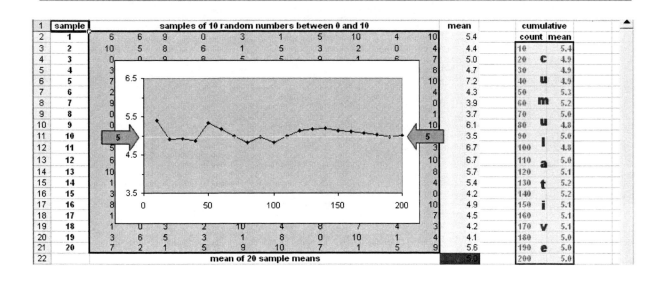

Estimating with a Normal Distribution

There are two different ways of looking at the problem of estimating with confidence:

> ➤ If the sample's mean were 7, what would the population's mean be if we kept sampling? This is where we use a sample to get an idea about the population.

> ➤ If the population's mean were 7, which range of means could we expect in its samples? This is more common in dealing with quality control and the like.

The mean actually measured in a sample is one out of several you could have found had you measured other subsets. To find out how far the possible means could deviate from the observed mean, we need to know the standard deviation of the means around the sampling distribution's mean.

Usually we only know the standard deviation of the sample distribution. Based on this, we estimate the standard deviation of the sampling distribution. This estimate of the SD of means is often called the *Standard Error*:

$$\text{Standard Error} = \text{StDev} / \text{Sqrt}(n) \text{ (or: } n-1 \text{ for very small samples)}$$

These are the steps to take (see Figure - 24):

1. Use the sample information after calculating the Standard Error (column D), based on the StDev (column C).

2. Calculate the Z-value (in column J) that comes with 2.5% for each tail (which is a total of 5% probability).

3. Calculate the confidence range .for either side (column K) – which is Z*StError.

4. Now we know with 95% confidence the minimum mean (column L) and the maximum mean (M) – also called the *confidence interval*.

Figure - 24

An example showing how to calculate confidence levels or limits, as well as confidence intervals

	A	B	C	D	E	F	G	H	I	J	K	L	M
1		SAMPLES						Confidence				Mean	
2	Feature	Mean	StDev	StErr	Count		Level	Error	2-tails	Z or t	Limit	Min	Max
3													
4			size over 30								Z		
5	Weight	4.15	0.32	0.05	35		95%	5%	2.5%	-1.96	-0.11	4.04	4.26
6											0.11	4.04	4.26
7													
8	pH	6.80	0.04	0.01	50		95%	5%	2.5%	-1.96	-0.01	6.79	6.81
9													

Figure - 25

A cumulative Normal Distribution for Z-values from −3 to +3

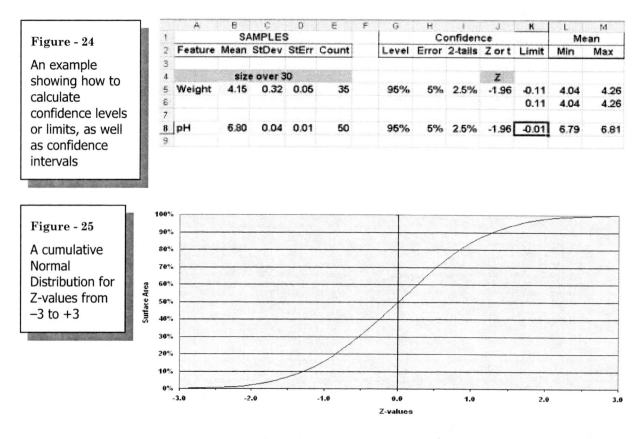

 Exercise 11.

Type the following in your spreadsheet:

➢ Number of cases is 90

➢ Mean of 19.01

➢ Standard deviation of 2.2

1. What is the Z-value for 2.5% probability?

2. What is the Standard Error for the Normal Distribution?

3. What are the limits to the left (at 2.5%) and to the right (at 97.5%) that we are willing to accept?

4. What is the minimum mean; what is the maximum mean?

5. How confident are we that the "real" mean is in between maximum and minimum?

6. How much risk are we willing to take?

7. Save your spreadsheet.

Estimating with a t-Distribution

If the samples are smaller than 30, you should use *t-scores* instead of *Z-scores*.

The Student's *t-Distribution* is a sampling distribution similar to the normal distribution but with a flatter and wider shape, depending on the sample's size. It works with t-scores (+) instead of Z-scores (– and +). However, a condition for using the t-Test is the assumption that the population has a normal distribution. The Z-test, on the other hand, does not come with this condition; however, the sample's size must be larger than 30 (see Table - 12).

TINV calculates the t-value for a specific probability, depending on the sample's size (expressed in degrees of freedom: n–1).

In Figure - 26, the limits are calculated based on a t-value because the sample size is below 30. Since t-values are always and only positive, they give you a two-tailed distribution.

 Tip:

To get a 2.5% one-tailed version, go for a 5% two-tailed distribution.

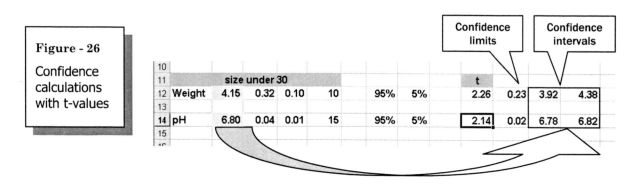

Figure - 26

Confidence calculations with t-values

<table>
<tr><td>Table - 12

Each test has its own conditions.</td><td></td><td>t</td><td>Z</td></tr>
</table>

	t	Z
Sample size	–	>30
Population	normal	–

Exercise 12.

This is the same data that you used in Exercise 11. However, this time you will only consider 24 cases instead of 90. Type the following in your spreadsheet:

➢ number of cases 24

➢ mean of 19.01

➢ standard deviation of 2.2

1. What is the t-value for 5% (tinv is basically two-tailed)?

2. What is the Standard Error for the t-Distribution?

3. What are the limits to the left (at 2.5%) and to the right (at 97.5%) that we are willing to accept?

4. What are the minimum and the maximum means?

5. How confident are we that the "real" mean is in between maximum and minimum?

6. How much risk are we willing to take?

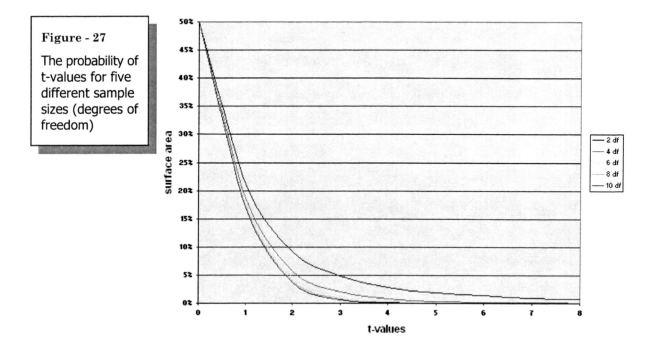

Figure - 27

The probability of t-values for five different sample sizes (degrees of freedom)

Estimating with a Binomial Distribution

What is the chance of "success" (p_{yes} = cases$_{yes}$ / cases$_{total}$) in the total population based on sample measurements? We can use Z-scores or t-scores to calculate, with a certain confidence, say 95%, what the limits are for p_{yes} in the total population. We therefore take a 5% risk of finding the "real p" outside the limits that we have set.

The main difference for a binomial distribution is the way we estimate the *Standard Error*:

$$\text{Standard Error} = \text{Sqrt}(p*(1-p)) / \text{Sqrt}(n) \quad \text{OR:} \quad = \text{Sqrt}(p*(1-p)*n)$$

II

Let's say we used three dichotomized groups (Figure - 28): head/tail, male/female, immune/not-immune. Based on the findings below, we can calculate p_{yes} plus the Standard Error. From this, we can deduce the limits by using Z-values (>30 cases).

Figure - 28

Calculations of confidence limits and intervals for some binomial cases

	A	B	C	D	E	F	G	H	I	J	K	L
1	Char	Yes	No	Total	p_{yes}			Trials	Find Yes	Exactly	At most	
2	Head	503	497	1000	0.50			10	10	0.10%	100.00%	
3												
4	Male	45	55	100	0.45			10	6	15.96%	89.80%	
5												
6	Immune	165	35	200	0.83			10	3	0.03%	0.04%	
7												
8												
9						StError		Level	Z	Limit	Min P_{yes}	Max P_{yes}
10	Head	500	500	1000	0.50	0.02		95%	-1.96	0.03	0.47	0.53
11												
12	Male	45	55	100	0.45	0.05		95%	-1.96	0.10	0.35	0.55
13												
14	Immune	165	35	200	0.83	0.03		95%	-1.96	0.05	0.77	0.88

Table - 13

Confidence intervals for two types of distributions with different sample sizes

Sample Size	Type	Confidence intervals
>30	x	x + (Z * (SD / √n))
	p	p + (Z * (√p*(1-p) / √n))
<30	x	x ± (t * (SD / √n))
	p	p ± (t * (√p*(1-p) / √n))

Exercise 13.

Refer to Figure - 29 below. We find 12 defects in a sample of 100 products.

1. What is the chance (p) of finding a defect?
2. What is the Standard Error?
3. What is the Z-value for a 95% confidence level?
4. What are the acceptable limits on either side of the mean?
5. What are the minimum and maximum chances of finding defects in the total population?

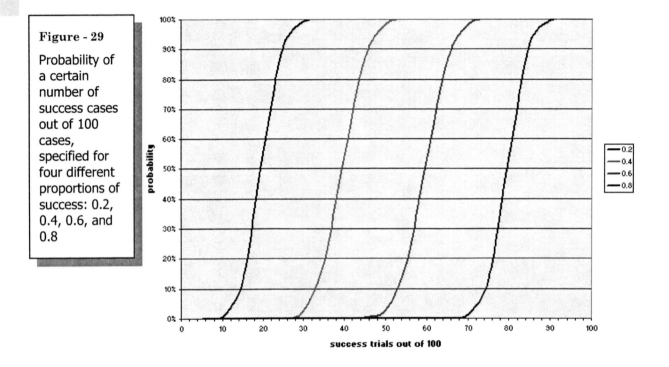

Figure - 29

Probability of a certain number of success cases out of 100 cases, specified for four different proportions of success: 0.2, 0.4, 0.6, and 0.8

Testing with Significance

Doing research is testing theories by means of experiments. However, all experiments are impacted by chance variation such as the (in-)accuracy and the (limited) number of measurements. So, we need statistical techniques to test how big a part chance plays in the outcome.

Here are two issues to consider:

➢ Is a sample's mean of 6 within the range of means expected for a population whose mean is 7?

➢ Can two samples with a mean of 6 and of 8 be drawn from the same population with a mean of 7?

In practice, we usually have two hypotheses:

🍶 *Null* hypothesis: All variation is due to random sampling variation.

🍶 Alternative hypothesis: All variation is due to some hypothetical factor

Next we need to set a limit (usually 95%):

🍶 Inside the limit: We accept the null hypothesis and declare the results random.

🍶 Outside the limit: We accept the alternative hypothesis and declare the results significant (one-tailed: 5%; two-tailed: 2*2.5%) or highly significant (2*1%).

The limit we set here depends on how much of a risk we are willing to take that our null rejection may be wrong. At a 5% significance level, we accept a 5% risk of rejecting a true null hypothesis. This risk can be at both the low end (2.5%) and the high end (2.5%) or at one end only (5%).

Note:

1% would usually be called highly significant. This percentage is often designated with p, especially in medical literature. In this book, we reserve p for binomial proportions.

Testing with Normal and t-Distribution

Usually, we want to check the observed mean as found in the sample against the expected mean from the population.

There may be several reasons for doing so:

➢ To test whether the sample is an instance of the population

➢ To find out whether a certain treatment of the sample made it different from another sample or from the population.

To check the observed mean, we can use Z-scores or t-scores to find out how far the difference is away from the mean. With samples smaller than 30, t-scores are much more reliable than Z-scores but they require the assumption of a normal distribution in the population.

Once again, we are dealing with two different hypotheses:

🍶 Null hypothesis: Differences are due to chance

🍶 Alternative hypothesis: Differences are due to the factor under investigation

	Figure - 30
	A t-test as to whether the difference between the observed mean of 35.3 and the expected mean of 33 is significant or rather random

	A	B	C	D	E
1	Measurements		Hypothesis: Observed = Expected		
2	30.3				
3	34.7			Observed	Expected
4	40.0		mean	35.3	33
5	36.1		stdev	4.2	
6	41.3		n	7	
7	34.5		level of probability	5%	
8	30.5		stderror	1.6	
9			actual t-value	1.5	
10			maximum t-value (TINV)	2.4	
11					

In the case of Figure - 30, the actual t-value is:

$$=\text{ABS} (\text{mean}_{observed} - \text{mean}_{expected}) / \text{StError}$$

Since the *actual* t-value (1.5) is less than the *critical* t-value (2.4 at the 5% level), the difference between the observed and the expected value is acceptable within the margin of 95%. Consequently, we accept the difference as random – and therefore not significant. In other words, we have no compelling reason to explain the difference by factors other than chance.

Figure - 31

A significance test for paired measurements or observations.

	A	B	C	D	E	F	G	H
1	**Strain**	**Treated**	**Non-treated**	**Diff.**		**Hypothesis: Observed = Expected**		
2	1	1.11	0.97	0.14				
3	2	3.77	4.33	-0.56				
4	3	5.94	5.35	0.59		mean of diff.	0.16	
5	4	2.90	2.30	0.60		stdev of diff.	0.45	
6	5	1.04	1.19	-0.15		n	6	
7	6	4.23	3.88	0.35		level of probability	5%	
8						stderror	0.19	
9						observed t-value	0.87	
10						maximum t-value	2.57	
11						verdict		

The story is rather similar when we are dealing with paired measurements (see Figure - 31). All that matters is the difference for each pair. To find out whether the *mean* of these differences is significant, calculate the observed t-value:

$$= \text{meandiff} / \text{StError}$$

And the verdict is that the differences are not significant because $t_{obs} < t_{crit}$.

The situation is different, though, when you need to deal with repeated measurements on different samples with different sizes. These are not paired samples like before!

The first problem is that you have to "pool" their standard deviations. This is done with a *pooled standard deviation*. A pooled standard deviation is an SD based on repeated measurements of several samples.

We need the following for all samples:

🧪 The SSD (the sum of the squared SDs) for each sample obtained: Use the function DEVSQ

🧪 Degrees of freedom: The sum of the df in each sample

🧪 A pooled SD: SQRT((SSD1 + SSD2 + ...)/df)

Next, you may need to compare all measurements found in different samples. This is where t-values come in again for each combination of two samples; however, this time the pooled SD becomes part of it:

$$=(\text{ABS} (X_1-X_2)/\text{PooledSD})*\text{SQRT} ((n_1*n_2)/(n_1+n_2))$$

 Tip:

A much easier way – if you have only <u>two</u> sets of data – is to use the TTEST function with its fourth argument set to "2" (for samples with equal variance).

Exercise 14.

In a sample of 25 cases, we find a mean pH of 6.79 with a standard deviation of 0.06. But we expected to find 6.81.

1. What is the standard error?

2. Are we going to use: a Z- or a t-value?

3. How far away is the difference between 6.79 and 6.81 from the mean in t-units?

4. What is the critical t-value at a 5% significance level?

5. Do we accept the null hypothesis (and reject a significant difference)?

Testing with a Binomial Distribution

Binomial testing is cumulative, so it is important to know how you want to test:

➤ At the <u>low</u> end only: one test to find the <u>lowest</u> acceptable number

➤ At the <u>high</u> end only: one test to find the <u>highest</u> acceptable number

➤ At <u>both</u> ends: a <u>combination</u> of these two tests

Which side(s) you want to test depends on your alternative hypothesis: Testing for a lower chance is checking at the lower end; testing for a higher chance means a check at the higher end.

The null hypothesis says there is NO difference – so p is 50%.

<table>
<tr><td rowspan="11">

Figure - 32

Three different significance tests based on a *Binomial Distribution*.

</td><td colspan="9">Test a sample of diseased cases for their ...</td></tr>
<tr><td></td></tr>
<tr><td>Treatment</td><td>Yes</td><td>No</td><td>Count</td><td>p_{yes}</td><td>Null: p</td><td>Alternative Hypo</td><td>95% sign.</td><td>Verdict</td></tr>
<tr><td>Vaccine</td><td>16</td><td>44</td><td>60</td><td>0.27</td><td>0.50</td><td>less disease: <50%</td><td>24</td><td>alternative</td></tr>
<tr><td></td></tr>
<tr><td>Sex</td><td>Yes</td><td>No</td><td>Count</td><td>p_{yes}</td><td>Null: p</td><td>Alternative Hypo</td><td>95% sign.</td><td>Verdict</td></tr>
<tr><td>Female</td><td>29</td><td>21</td><td>50</td><td>0.58</td><td>0.50</td><td>more disease: >50%</td><td>31</td><td>null</td></tr>
<tr><td></td></tr>
<tr><td>Diet</td><td>Yes</td><td>No</td><td>Count</td><td>p_{yes}</td><td>Null: p</td><td>Alternative Hypo</td><td>95% sign.</td><td>Verdict</td></tr>
<tr><td>Normal</td><td>35</td><td>45</td><td>80</td><td>0.44</td><td>0.50</td><td rowspan="2">some connection</td><td>31</td><td rowspan="2">null</td></tr>
<tr><td></td><td></td><td></td><td></td><td></td><td></td><td>49</td></tr>
</table>

In Figure - 32, the first case is based on a one-tailed test for the <u>lowest</u> critical number, because the alternative hypothesis assumes fewer cases of disease for vaccine-treated individuals. The second case is also one-tailed but for the <u>highest</u> critical number, because we are testing whether females are more susceptible to a certain disease. The third case needs a two-tailed test, since we assume there is some connection – in either direction.

The function you need in the cells below the 95% significance cell is CRITBINOM. This function allows you to determine the critical value for a 95% significance level and is cumulative.

Exercise 15.

Someone tosses a coin 50 times; we find tails only 10 times. Enter this information into your spreadsheet.

1. What is p for having tails?
2. What is p according to the null hypothesis?
3. To find out whether 20% is extremely low, how should we test: at the 5% level, 95% level, or both?
4. What is the minimum number of "tails cases" we accept?
5. Is it statistically reasonable to accuse this person of "manipulating" the coin?

Testing with a Chi-Square Distribution

If you need to compare an *observed frequency* distribution in the sample with an *expected frequency* distribution in the population, you can use the *Chi Square Distribution*.

This test allows you to decide whether a given sample was drawn from a population with a given distribution.

We have two hypotheses:

➢ Null hypothesis: they are identical (or close enough)

➢ Alternative hypothesis: they are most likely different – due to the factor under investigation

CHIINV returns the corresponding Chi-value for a certain degree of freedom. Tests are one-tailed. CHIDIST returns the probability of getting a specific Chi-value.

The graph of Figure - 33 shows the probability of finding specific Chi-values for certain degrees of freedom: (rows – 1) * (columns – 1).

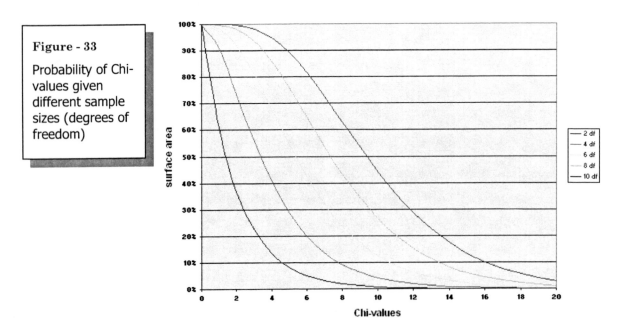

Figure - 33

Probability of Chi-values given different sample sizes (degrees of freedom)

Expected frequencies can be based on the assumption that there is no connection between the categories – in other words, each section should be populated proportionally. For instance: The proportion of <u>A-being-C</u> should be the same as the proportion of <u>B-being-C</u>.

In section AC, we would expect either:

Total-A / GrandTotal * Total-C
(= 57/84*35 = 23.75)
or
Total-C / GrandTotal * Total-A
(= 35/84*57 = 23.75)

Table - 14

Totals and grand total for A, B, C, and D

Observed	C	D	Total
A	20	37	57
B	15	12	27
Total	35	49	84

The Excel function CHITEST is capable of calculating the probability of having a set of observed frequencies against a set of expected frequencies. If that probability is in the significance range, we reject the Null hypothesis and go for a significant difference.

Figure - 34

After calculating the expected frequencies for a set of observed frequencies, the CHITEST function can find the probability.

	Observed frequencies:				Hypothesis of Independence	
1						
2					CHITEST	7.56%
3		Sick	Cured	TOTAL	5% sign.	accept
4	Serum	20	37	57		
5	Placebo	15	12	27	maximum CHIINV	3.841
6	TOTAL	35	49	84	actual CHIINV	3.158
7					CHIDIST	0.076
8						
9	Expected frequencies (if indep.):					
10						
11		Sick	Cured	TOTAL		
12	Serum	23.75	33.25	57		
13	Placebo	11.25	15.75	27		
14	TOTAL	35	49	84		

Expected frequencies can also be based on a theoretical assumption, such as: Each category is populated according to some Mendelian law. You can test your hypothesis with *Chi-Square*. For example: From crossing AaBb x aabb, we expect 25% AaBb, 25% Aabb, 25% aaBb, 25% aabb (see Figure - 35).

Figure - 35

Expected frequencies are based here on a Mendelian hypothesis, which is tested against a Null hypothesis.

	Observed frequencies:				Hypothesis of Independence	
1						
2					CHITEST	0.82%
3	AaBb x aabb	*Bb*	*bb*	TOTAL	5% sign.	reject
4	*Aa*	15	21	36		
5	*aa*	20	32	52	maximum CHIINV	3.841
6	TOTAL	35	53	88	actual CHIINV	7.000
7					CHIDIST	0.82%
8						
9	Expected frequencies (no linkage):					
10						
11	AaBb x aabb	*Bb* 50%	*bb* 50%	TOTAL		
12	*Aa* 50%	22	22	44		
13	*aa* 50%	22	22	44		
14	TOTAL	44	44	88		

Chi-Distribution has a huge advantage over other distributions in that your population doesn't have to be equally distributed nor is an equal variance required. Take, for instance, the example shown in Table - 15:

<table>
<tr><td rowspan="6">

Table - 15

Groups of different sizes and different ethnicity were measured for cholesterol levels. The means and standard deviations differed widely.
</td><td colspan="4">**Cholesterol** Measurements</td></tr>
<tr><td>Ethnicity</td><td>X</td><td>SD</td><td>n</td></tr>
<tr><td>African-Americans</td><td>198</td><td>26</td><td>75</td></tr>
<tr><td>Caucasians</td><td>167</td><td>14</td><td>65</td></tr>
<tr><td>Hispanics</td><td>175</td><td>9</td><td>60</td></tr>
<tr><td>Native Americans</td><td>159</td><td>5</td><td>45</td></tr>
</table>

The Z-test will not do, but the Chi-test will. All you need to do is to transform your data by creating your own categories, so you can use the Chi-Distribution for frequencies.

<table>
<tr><td rowspan="6">

Table - 16

The figures that Table - 16 is based on have to be changed into frequency figures according to newly created categories.
</td><td colspan="4">**Cholesterol** Measurements</td></tr>
<tr><td>Ethnicity</td><td><160</td><td>160-190</td><td>>190</td></tr>
<tr><td>African-Americans</td><td>5</td><td>40</td><td>30</td></tr>
<tr><td>Caucasians</td><td>20</td><td>30</td><td>15</td></tr>
<tr><td>Hispanics</td><td>15</td><td>30</td><td>15</td></tr>
<tr><td>Native Americans</td><td>20</td><td>15</td><td>10</td></tr>
</table>

Now we can compare the matrix of observations found in Table - 16 with a calculated matrix of expectations, so the *ChiTest* function can be applied. In this case, ChiTest would return 0.00026, which implies that, in this highly imaginary case, the difference between these ethnic groups is highly significant!

Exercise 16.

We want to test whether employees are sick more often (on an average) on certain weekdays. These are the data for your spreadsheet:
Mon 125, Tue 97, Wed 92, Thu 90, and Fri 111

1. Add data to your spreadsheet based on the null hypothesis.

2. How many degrees of freedom?

3. What is the probability of the observed range versus the expected range?

4. What is the critical Chi-value at a 5% level?

5. What is the actual Chi-value at a 7.5% level?

6. Is there a significant preference for certain weekdays at the 5% level?

Testing with F-Distributions

The F-distribution is appropriate for studying the difference between two *variances*. Just as using the sampling distribution of t or Z can compare two means, two variances can be compared by using the sampling distribution of *F*.

F is the ratio between the larger and the smaller variance of two data sets (not reversed, so always >0). The rest is very similar to t- and Z-testing:

🧪 FDIST() finds the two-tailed probability for F based on the degrees of freedom for each data set.

🧪 FINV() finds the critical F-value for a certain probability (say, 5%) with two figures for degrees of freedom.

🧪 FTEST() finds the one-tailed probability for both data sets.

Variance is calculated by using VAR(): Variance = SD^2

$$F = VAR^{larger} / VAR^{smaller}$$

Table - 17 An F-test can determine whether or not the two test samples compared here have different variances.	**Test1**	**Test2**	**Comparing variances (SD²) instead of means**		
	1.11	0.97	F is the ratio between large and small variance		
	3.77	4.33	SD1	1.90	
	5.94	5.35	SD2	1.56	
	2.90	2.30	Var1	3.60	
	1.04	1.19	Var2	2.42	
	4.23	3.88	F: Ratio L/S	1.49	
		3.12	FDIST	31%	Two-tailed (x2)
		4.09	FINV	3.97	Null
			FTEST	61%	One-tailed

In Table - 17, you could test whether a difference in temperature (say, low in Test1, and high in Test2) creates a greater variability of readings. What is your verdict?

> ➢ If you want to test whether these two samples significantly differ in *variance* (in either direction), you would use a two-tailed test. Since 1.49 is lower than the critical value 3.97, you would stick with the Null hypothesis.

> ➢ If you want to test whether the low temperature creates a larger *variance*, you go for the one-tailed test. Again you cannot find a significant difference (61% > 5%).

A related technique is called *analysis of variance*. This technique allows us to distinguish systematic differences between sample groups (as in mean) from the chance variation found within each group by computing an F-value. It uses the variance of sample means to estimate the variance of the population.

We use this technique to test the Null hypothesis – which says that means from several samples are equal (drawn from populations with the same mean).

We use the difference among sample means to estimate the population's variance. However, the assumption is that the population has a normal distribution. Differences between sample means are small if samples are from the same population.

	Test1	Test2	Test3
	1.11	3.77	0.97
	3.77	5.94	4.33
	5.94	2.90	5.35
	2.90	5.35	2.30
	1.04	2.30	1.19
	4.23	1.19	3.88
		1.11	3.12
		3.77	4.09
		0.97	
		4.33	

Table - 18

The Analysis of Variance uses the variance of sample means to determine whether the means of several samples are equal.

Could you use the t-test for the data in Table - 18 instead? You certainly could, but you would need to make three comparisons: Columns 1-2, 1-3, 2-3. Because each comparison has a 5% chance of error, you would have substantially more than a 5% chance of at least one error.

The Analysis of Variance, on the other hand, makes only one comparison: variance$_{B-G}$ (between-groups) as a ratio of variance$_{W-G}$ (within-groups)

$$F = \text{b-g variance} / \text{w-g variance}$$

🜑 Between-groups variance is the variance of the groups means

🜑 Within-groups variance is the variance of all group elements

🜑 Conditions include similar variances and normal distribution

The calculations in the background are involved, so it might be easier for this occasion to use the Analysis ToolPak (see page 17): *Tools / Data Analysis / Anova: Single Factor*. Be aware, though, that the results do not update!

Table - 19 shows the results based on the data in Table - 18:

Table - 19

The Analysis Toolpak provides a single-factor Analysis of Variance (Anova) tool.

Anova: Single Factor						
Summary						
Groups	*Count*	*Sum*	*Average*	*Variance*		
Column 1	6	18.99	3.165	3.60195		
Column 2	10	31.63	3.163	3.147134		
Column 3	8	25.23	3.15375	2.423741		
Anova						
Source of Variation	*SS*	*df*	*MS*	*F*	*P-value*	*F crit*
Between Groups	0.000548	2	0.000274	0.0001	0.999909	3.466795
Within Groups	63.30015	21	3.014293			

SS is the *Sum of Squares:* ($\Sigma(x-x_m)^2$). Instead of using variances, we use the Sum of Squares whenever the sample groups are not of equal size.

Table - 19 leads us to the conclusion that there is no significant difference between the three series of measurements as to their variance, since F (0.0001) is far below F-critical (3.47).

Very often, we need to study the combined effects of two variables. Your ideal tool to do so is a two-factor Analysis of Variance.

Let's say that we count the number of colonies on Petri dishes under two sets of conditions:

> Difference in pH (factor 1)

> Difference in nutrient level (factor 2)

In Table - 20, we have six samples (s1-s6), each containing 10 dishes. In each of the 10 dishes per sample, the numbers of colonies were counted. Let us use the Analysis Toolpak again – this time with Anova's Two-Factor with Replication (based on the total table in the left section of Table - 20, and 10 rows per sample).

Table - 20 The Analysis Toolpak also provides a two-factor Analysis of Variance (Anova).

		pH<6	pH 6-8	pH>8	Anova: Two Factor with Replication				
		1	4	6					
		2	5	7	Summary	pH<6	pH 6-8	pH>8	Total
		2	5	7	<2000 mg				
		3	6	8	Count	10.0	10.0	10.0	30.0
<2000 mg	S1	3	S2 6	S3 8	Sum	30.0	60.0	80.0	170.0
		3	6	8	Average	3.0	6.0	8.0	5.7
		3	6	8	Variance	1.3	1.3	1.3	5.6
		4	7	9					
		4	7	9	>2000 mg				
		5	8	10	Count	10.0	10.0	10.0	30.0
		5	3	0	Sum	70.0	50.0	20.0	140.0
		6	4	1	Average	7.0	5.0	2.0	4.7
		6	4	1	Variance	1.3	1.3	1.3	5.6
		7	5	2					
>2000 mg	S4	7	S5 5	S6 2	Total				
		7	5	2	Count	20.0	20.0	20.0	
		7	5	2	Sum	100.0	110.0	100.0	
		8	6	3	Average	5.0	5.5	5.0	
		8	6	3	Variance	5.5	1.5	10.7	
		9	7	4					

ANOVA						
Source of Variation	*SS*	*df*	*MS*	*F*	*P-value*	*F crit*
Sample/Rows	15.0	1.0	15.0	11.3	0.0	4.0
Columns	3.3	2.0	1.7	1.2	0.3	3.2
Interaction	250.0	2.0	125.0	93.8	0.0	3.2
Within	72.0	54.0	1.3			

There are four SS calculations this time:

> One for between-rows (B-R) variance (15)

➢ One for between-cols (B-C) variance (3.3)

➢ One for interaction (250)

➢ One for within-group (W-G) variance (72)

➢ None for between-groups (B-G) variance (268)

What is *Interaction*? The B-G SS is usually larger than the combination of B-R SS plus B-C SS. The remaining part of the difference between cells is due to the combined effects of rows and columns – which is the interaction of both variables.

Which differences are significant here? Only the differences for the factor nutrient level (rows: 11.3 > 4.0) and the interaction between both factors (93.8 > 3.2). But the differences for pH are not significant (1.2 < 3.2).

A word of caution, though. If we were to use both significant F-ratios at the same time, we would run a risk higher than 5% of being wrong! So the question is, which of these two significant F-ratios counts the most?

The answer depends on our alternative hypothesis!

🧪 If we are interested in the main effects – i.e., differences in rows (or columns) – we want to know which pH (or which level) is best.

🧪 If we are interested in their interaction, we want to know the best combination of pH and level.

The analysis of variance can become more complicated when going into more variables and categories. We will leave this issue for books on statistical analysis.

Exercise 17.

We have two samples with the following characteristics:
n = 10; x = 8.8; sd = 12
n = 12; x = 12.7; sd = 5

1. What is the F-value for both samples?

2. What is the critical value for 1% significance?

3. Are both samples equally variable?

Exercise 18.

Assume we measured the effect of different dosages of a certain drug (in ng/ml):

10 ng	6.8	7.1	6.9	7.2	
20 ng	7.1	7.1	7.2	6.9	7.3
30 ng	7.7	7.2	7.8	7.6	

1. Apply the Analysis ToolPak.

2. Is the difference in dosage significant for the results?

3. How likely is this combination of data?

Table - 21 The following books provide detailed information about the algorithms and methods used to create the Microsoft Excel analysis tools and statistical functions.

Strum, Robert D., and Donald E. Kirk. First Principles of Discrete Systems and Digital Signal Processing. Reading, Mass.: Addison-Wesley Publishing Company, 1988.

Abramowitz, Milton, and Irene A. Stegun, eds. Handbook of Mathematical Functions, with Formulas, Graphs, and Mathematical Tables. Washington, D.C.: U.S. Government Printing Office, 1972.

Box, George E.P., William G. Hunter, and J. Stuart Hunter. Statistics for Experimenters: An Introduction to Design, Data Analysis, and Model Building. New York: John Wiley and Sons, 1978.

Devore, Jay L. Probability and Statistics for Engineering and the Sciences. 4th ed. Wadsworth Publishing, 1995.

McCall, Robert B. Fundamental Statistics for the Behavioral Sciences. 5th ed. New York: Harcourt Brace Jovanovich, 1990.

Press, William H., Saul A. Teukolsky, William T. Vetterling, and Brian P. Flannery. Numerical Recipes in C: The Art of Scientific Computing. second ed. New York: Cambridge University Press, 1992.

Sokal, Robert R., and F. James Rohlf. Biometry: The Principles and Practice of Statistics in Biological Research. second ed. New York: W. H. Freeman, 1995.

II

Exercise 19.

Mark the correct boxes in Table - 22 :

Table - 22

This is an overview of the most important statistical functions in Excel.

	type X in the right box CSA	STANDARDIZE	NORMSINV	NORMDIST	NORMSDIST	TINV	TDIST	TTEST	BINOMDIST	CRITBINOM	CHIINV	CHIDIST	CHITEST
2	Cumulative probability of a specific mean		X										
3	Distance from mean in StDev units (Z)												
4	Probability for a specific Z-score												
5	Probability for X successes in Y trials												
6	Probability for a specific t-score												
7	Probability for a specific Chi-score												
8	Probability for 2 sets of frequencies												
9	Probability of paired sets of data												
10	Z-score for a specific probability												
11	t-score for a specific probability												
12	Chi-score for a specific probability												
13	Citical value for a specific p (binom.)												

Exercise 20.

What is the correct distribution test for each of these cases:

1. 15 sets of separated identical twins were tested for IQ. One twin of each set was adopted by a family; the other was placed in an institution. Is there significance?

2. 85 out of 120 have acquired immunity from a vaccine. Is the vaccine effective?

3. Four baits, each with a different pheromone, catch 33, 21, 45, 25 mosquitoes, respectively. Is there a significant difference in performance?

4. Does calibration of the same 50 samples on machine A and machine B result in significantly different readings?

5. 75 mosquitoes were caught with pheromone 1, and 115 with pheromone 2. Is pheromone 2 more effective?

6. 12 plants treated with growth hormone measure 1.25 m, whereas 15 without treatment measure 0.94 m. Is the difference significant?

7. Among 20 Blacks, 25 Asians, and 31 Indians, we find 9, 4, and 5 persons with sickle cell anemia. Is there a significant difference?

8. Does the use of two different techniques in measuring the same sample 10x give us the same measurements?

Chapter III: Plotting Graphs

Science calls them *Graphs*. Business calls them *Charts*, so Excel calls them Charts, too. But they are basically the same thing.

Charts are based on tables with *categories* (usually in the rows) and *series of values* (usually in the columns; see Figure - 36). They typically display the categories on the <u>horizontal</u> axis (X-axis) and the values on the <u>vertical</u> axis (Y-axis).

If you were to display the data in the table shown in Figure - 36 in a graph like that shown in Figure - 37, the first table column would be considered categories, and not X-values.

Figure - 36

A simple example of a table holding categories and series of values for a graph

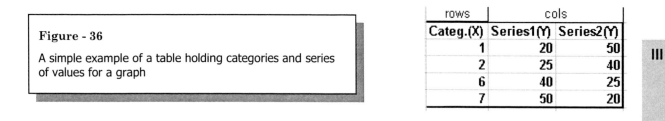

III

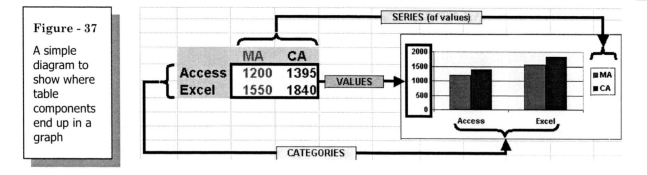

Figure - 37

A simple diagram to show where table components end up in a graph

Types of Charts

Basically, there are four different types of graphs:

- *Pie* charts display only one series of values; for other series, you need another pie (or one set of concentric "donuts"). Combined, all of the values in this one series of values make up 100% of the pie.

- *Column* and *Bar* charts can hold many series of values. The labels of those series are shown in the legend. The horizontal axis displays categories (even if they are values – so 1 would actually be "1").

- *Line* charts are very similar to the previous group. Again, the horizontal axis holds categories (names or labels) but never real values.

- *XY* or *Scatter* charts may look like Line charts, but they have real values on the horizontal axis – which changes it into an X-axis.

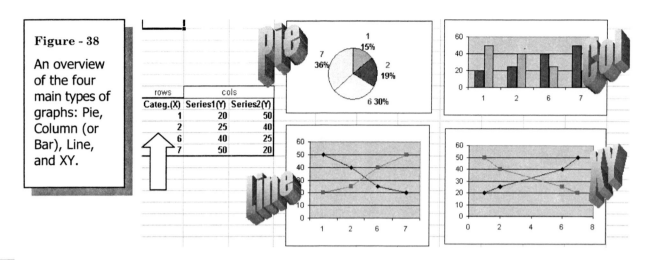

Figure - 38

An overview of the four main types of graphs: Pie, Column (or Bar), Line, and XY.

In a Line chart, the first table column holds categories (text). In an *XY* chart, however, the first table column would hold X-values (numeric). If you want to combine graphs types into one graph, they must be compatible:

🜛 A Pie chart is unique (and very limited)

🜛 A Line chart can be combined with a Column chart – both display categories

🜛 An XY chart cannot be combined with the other types

Usually, a click inside the table (delineated by an empty row and column at the end) plus a click on the Chart Wizard button (on the Standard Toolbar) will give you the graph you want. The rest is a matter of fine-tuning or fixing problems.

Manipulating Graphs

This table provides a convenient list of changes you may want to make to your graphs along with an easy way to make those changes.

Table - 23 Ways and means of making changes to graphs

Objective	Means
Change the type of the <u>entire</u> chart	Chart menu – Change Type
Change the type of <u>one series</u> only	R-Click on the series – Change Type
Add new rows/cols from table to chart	Chart menu – Add Data
Shift series from rows to categories (or reverse)	Chart menu – Source Data – Data Range tab
Add or remove categories or series	Chart menu – Source Data – Series tab
Change the order for all series of values	R-Click on a series – Format Data Series – Series Order tab
Put a data series on a secondary axis	R-Click on the series – Format Data Series – Axis tab

Objective	Means
Change the scale of either axis	R-Click on that axis – Format the Axis – **Scale tab**
Add titles to chart and/or axis	Chart menu – Chart Options – Titles tab
Add the chart to the table (or away from it)	Chart menu – Location
Add the table to the chart (or remove it)	Chart menu – Chart Options – Data Table tab
Fix the axis	R-Click on the axis – Format Axis Scale tab: Major/Minor Patterns tab: Minor tick – *Chart / Options / Gridlines*
Add Y-error bars	R-Click on the series – Format Data Series – **Bars** tab: % or *StDev*
Regulate Gap and Overlap for bars and columns	R-Click on the series – Format Data Series – Options tab
Regulate the kind of lines in Line or XY charts	Chart menu OR R-Click – Change Type – Choose different subset
Move the vertical axis from the center to the left	R-Click on the axis – Format Axis – Patterns: Tick Labels Low (and: Lines None)

This is the big difference between the Line and XY types of graphs (see Figure - 39):

- Line type uses categories on the X-axis (value 4 is missing here), whereas
- XY type uses real values on the X-axis (so value 4 shows no data).

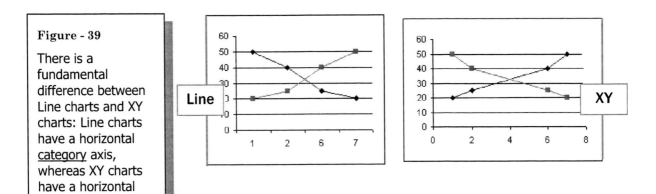

Figure - 39

There is a fundamental difference between Line charts and XY charts: Line charts have a horizontal <u>category</u> axis, whereas XY charts have a horizontal <u>value</u> axis.

A graph updates when its table changes – unless you add rows or columns at the very <u>end</u> of the table.

When you do add new rows or columns to the end of the table, there are at least three different ways of adding them also to the graph:

> ➢ Copy the cells from the table; click inside the graph; choose Paste Special.

> ➢ Click inside the graph; choose Add Data from the Chart menu.

> ➢ Click inside the graph; choose Source Data from the Chart menu; go the Series tab (the second tab).

Of these three options, the Series tab in Source Data is the most powerful because it can add, change, or delete both series information and category information. When the Chart Wizard doesn't deliver what you expected, you can most likely fix your problems here.

In order to fix the appearance of a graph, you need to know a few basic rules:

> 🧪 Clicking in a graph's blank space selects or activates the chart

> 🧪 Clicking on one column selects all columns of that specific series of values

> 🧪 Clicking again on the same column selects only that particular column

> 🧪 R-Clicking in all previous cases also gives you proper menu choices

Adding an extra axis

Often, you may want an additional axis for values that have a scale different from the other values. Say, you want to add pH values to your graph (Figure - 40). Because they are of a different dimension, you want them displayed on a different axis. To do so, R-Click on that series of values. Then select / *Format the Data Series / Axis-tab*: ⊙ *Secondary Axis.*

Figure - 40

The fourth series of values (pH) uses values of a different proportion. These values call for a secondary vertical axis.

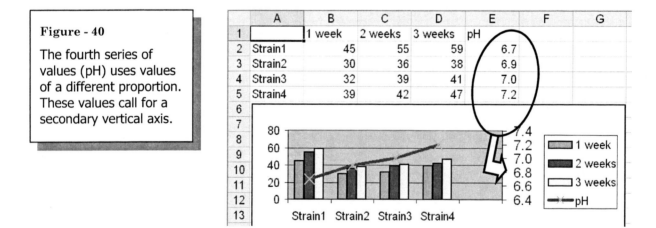

The same phenomenon occurs when comparing incremental values with cumulative values: Because their scales are of different proportions, we need two Y-axes (Figure - 41).

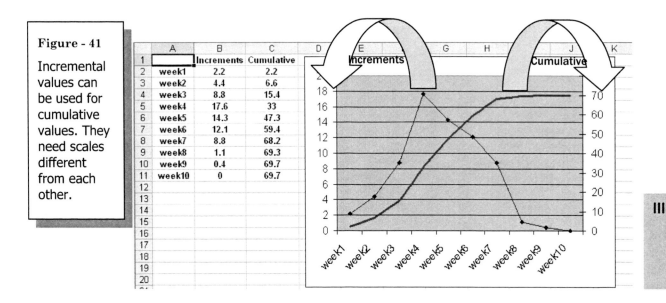

Figure - 41

Incremental values can be used for cumulative values. They need scales different from each other.

III

Line Charts versus XY Charts

When you use a table holding only columns of numbers (as in Figure - 42), the Wizard comes up with a correct graph if you create an XY chart.

Had you chosen a Line type chart instead, the Wizard would have made the wrong move: It would assume that you have <u>two</u> series of values, so the categories are missing. Therefore, the Wizard would create its own categories: 1, 2, 3 ...

How do you fix this problem?

Figure - 42

The Chart Wizard assumes there are two series of values here, so it creates a fake category axis.

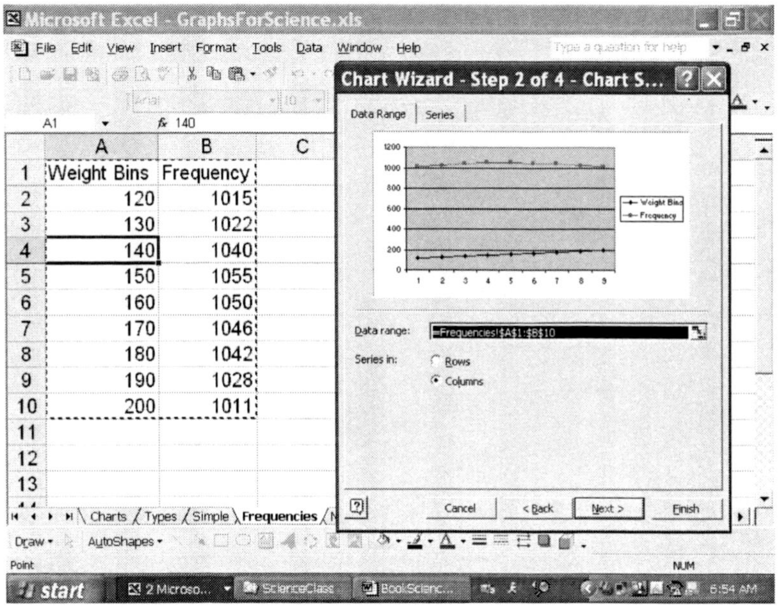

Obviously, we need to make some adjustments (see Figure - 43):

1. In the Source Data box, move from the Data Range tab to the Series tab. This is the place where you can control your own categories and series of values.

2. Remove Weight Bins as a Series of Values.

3. Use the Weight Bins values as Category Labels, instead.

Figure - 43

Source Data can be fixed in the Source Data dialog box after switching to the Series tab.

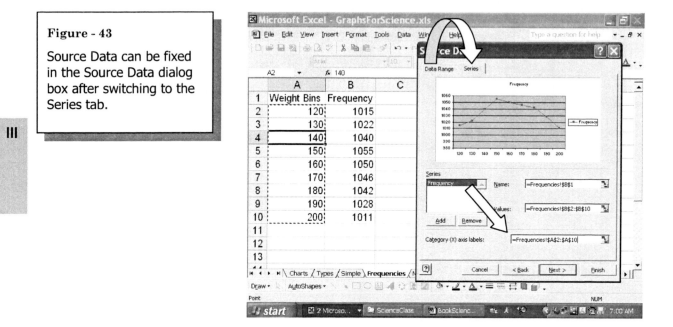

Using Error Bars

Error Bars are a great tool for a visual representation of Standard Deviations.

This is what you need to do:

1. R-Click on Series: */ Format Series / Y-Error-Bars tab / ⊙ Custom: SDs*

2. SD per Strain: *⊙ Series in Cols / Add Means as Line Chart / Error Bars on Mean:* F2:F4

3. SD per Week: *⊙ Series in Rows / Add Means as Line / Error Bars on Mean*: B6:D6

4. SD for Strain1: *R-Click on Strain1 / Format Series / Error Bars:* F2

Figure - 44

If a table includes Standard Deviations, they can be displayed as error-bars to the means – either for a specific mean or for all means (per row or per column).

	1 week	2 weeks	3 weeks	MEAN	SD
Strain1	0.45	0.55	0.70	0.57	0.13
Strain2	0.30	0.34	0.39	0.34	0.05
Strain3	0.32	0.37	0.43	0.37	0.06
MEAN	0.36	0.42	0.51		
SD	0.08	0.11	0.17		

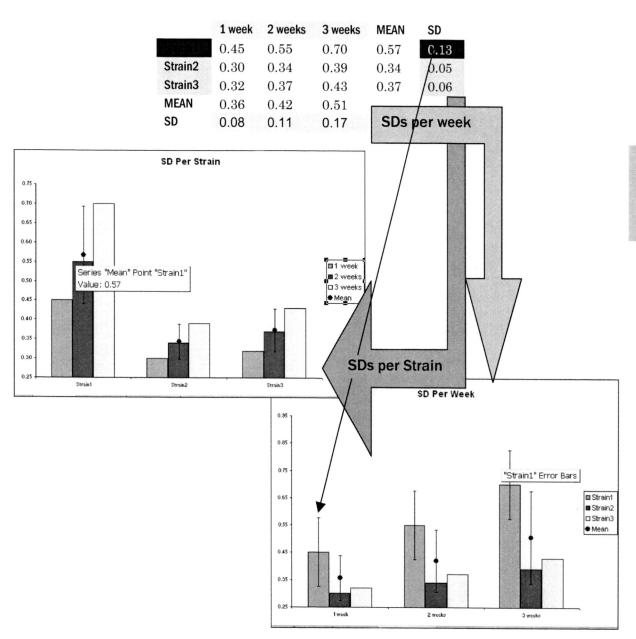

At other times, you may want more specific bars. Let's say you have the data in Figure - 45.

Figure - 45

The left section holds observed and predicted values for Y, plus their difference, which is visually plotted in the right section.

X	Y_{obs}	Y_{pred}	$Y_{obs} - Y_{pred}$
0.5	0.50	0.35	0.15
0.8	0.52	0.60	-0.08
1.2	1.05	0.92	0.13
1.7	1.22	1.33	-0.11
2.3	1.68	1.82	-0.14
2.9	2.04	2.31	-0.27
3.5	3.12	2.80	0.32

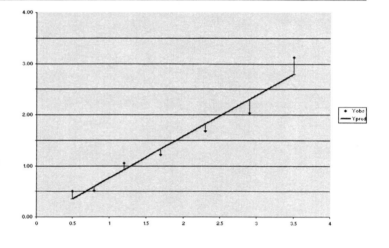

This is how the calculations shown in Figure - 45 were done:

1. Column C holds a prediction based on a calculated slope and intercept:
   =0.8154*A2 - 0.0556.

2. Column D holds the residuals.

3. Create an XY graph for columns A-C.

4. Make column B show as dots.

5. Make column C show as a straight line.

6. R-Click on this line, choose Format.

7. Go to the Error Bars tab.

8. Place D2:D8 in the + section of custom.

Exercise 21.

1. Plot a graph from the table created in Exercise 3. (See page 16.) Which type of chart do you need?

2. Adjust each axis until it looks like Figure - 46.

Figure - 46

Cumulative Normal Distribution

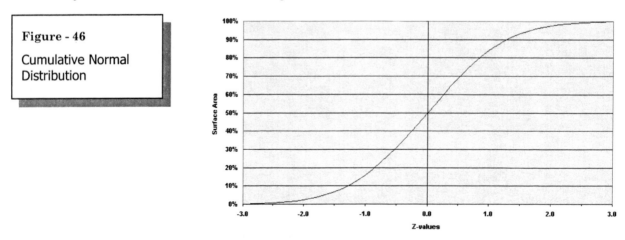

Exercise 22.

1. Plot a graph from the table created in Exercise 7. (See page 20.)
2. Make the graph look like Figure - 47.

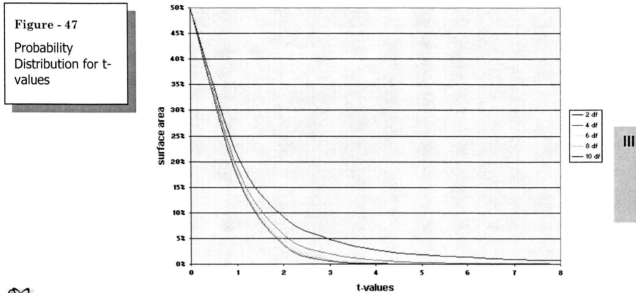

Figure - 47

Probability Distribution for t-values

Exercise 23.

1. Plot a graph from the table created in Exercise 10. (See page 22.)
2. Make the graph look like Figure - 48.

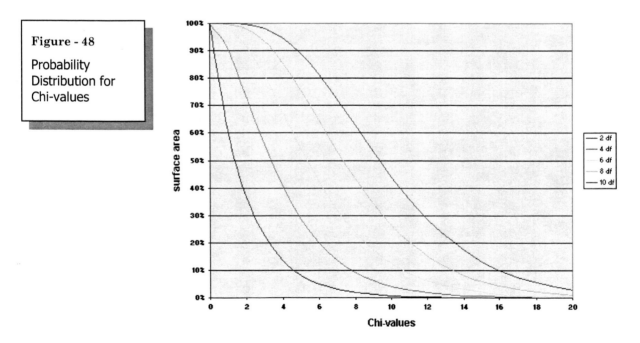

Figure - 48

Probability Distribution for Chi-values

Using Histograms

Histograms are Column-type graphs. They usually show frequencies found for specific bins or categories. Since graphs of the Column type display categories (and not values) on the horizontal axis, you probably want to make sure that the numbers used on the category axis have the same interval.

You may want to add a smooth Line of expected frequencies to the graph, perhaps based on an ideal normal distribution. To do so, you need to add another series of data with a (smooth) Line type. The Column type and Line type don't clash with each other because they each have an axis with category labels (and not values).

Figure - 49

The figure to the left provides frequencies for certain categories, which are displayed in the histogram to the right (plotted as a Column graph). Later, a second series of values based on Normal Distribution values was added and plotted as a Line graph.

1	Weight Bins	Frequency
2	120	1015
3	130	1022
4	140	1040
5	150	1055
6	160	1050
7	170	1046
8	180	1042
9	190	1028
10	300	1011

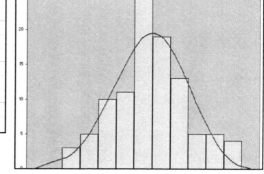

When using a table such as that shown for a histogram in Figure - 49, be prepared for some trouble:

If you choose a Column type, Excel will detect <u>two</u> series of values, and <u>no</u> categories. Here's what to do:

1. Go to *Source Data / Series* and delete the series Weight Bins.

2. Place the values of Weight Bins in the Categories box

3. Add the second column of values again and change its type to (smooth) Line.

4. Alternatively, you could add another column of values to the table, and use those for the Line graph.

In order to make the columns come closer together, you need to set the *Gap* property: R-Click on the Column series / *Format the Data Series* / *Options tab:* Set Gap to zero.

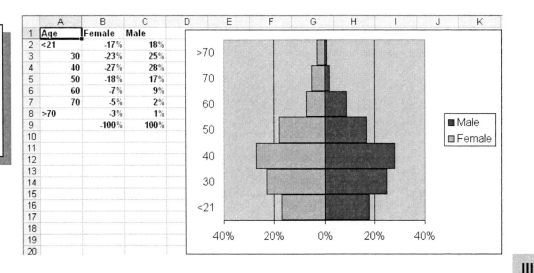

Figure - 50

A comparative histogram requires some additional techniques.

The example shown in Figure - 50 is a *comparative* histogram. It looks like a regular histogram, but it requires some different techniques:

1. Make sure the left series of values contains <u>negative</u> values.

2. Select *Bar* type and *Clustered* subtype.

3. Give the horizontal axis a customized format: 0%; 0%; 0%.

4. Format the Y-axis on the Patterns tab: Tick *Mark Labels* ⊙ *Low*.

5. Format the Data Series on the Options tab: *Overlap* 100 and *Gap Width* 0.

Exercise 24.

1. Use the Random number generator to create 100 random numbers according to a normal distribution with a mean of 10 and a standard deviation of 0.5.

2. Calculate the mean and standard deviation of these 100 numbers.

3. Create 13 equivalent frequency bins: from 8.50 and 8.75 up to 11.25 and 11.50.

4. Use the FREQUENCY function to calculate how many numbers each bin contains (do not hit Enter to accept the function but use Ctrl+Shift+Enter, instead).

5. Use the NormDist function to find out how many numbers each bin should hold if "ideal."

6. Create a Smooth Line graph with the bins are on the horizontal axis. Plot the observed and the expected frequencies on the vertical axis.

7. Change the type of the expected frequencies to column.

8. Set the gap between the columns to the value zero.

Configuring Default Graphs

By default, the Chart Wizard comes up with a Column chart of the first subtype and specific colors for all series of values (left panel in Figure - 51). If you press *F11* while you are in a table, the default chart will automatically pop up for that table.

> **Figure - 51**
>
> Three different shots for Chart Types. The first shot is part of the Wizard. The second and third shots comes from the Chart Type menu, but they show two different tabs: Standard Types and Custom Types.

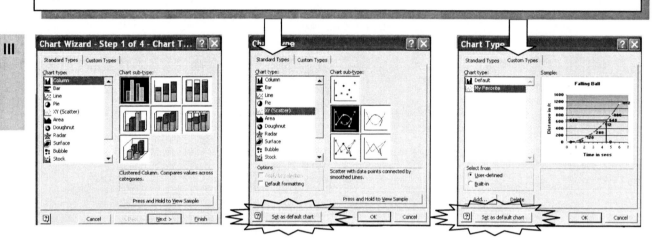

If you work more often with XY graphs than with Column graphs, you may want to set the XY type as a <u>default</u> type (middle panel in Figure - 51). What steps do you need to take?

1. First, you must create a graph (of any type).
2. While you are in the graph (not in the table!), select *Chart / Chart Type*.
3. Select the type and subtype of your choice.
4. Hit the *Set as Default Chart* button at the bottom.
5. Switch to the *Custom Types* tab.
6. Select ⊙ *User-Defined* and notice the default chart setting (right panel). Whenever you are in a table and hit the F11 key, this default chart pops up.

If you would like more specific formatting for your graph, just create a graph to your liking and then go through the following steps (right panel in Figure - 51):

1. While in the graph of your choice, select *Chart / Chart Type*.
2. Go to the *Custom Types* tab.
3. Select ⊙ *User-Defined*.
4. Hit the *Add* button and give your type a new name. Notice the new name in the listing.
5. Optional: You can make the new type default by hitting the *Set as Default* button (only then will F11 give you the formatted graph).

Putting Inserts in Graphs

Inserts are usually based on *interpolation*: In the graph, you want to mark a specific point on the curve that may not have been measured, but is interpolated.

Inserts Based on Formulas

Let us take the graph of Figure - 52 as an example. In this case, the series of values was created by using an exponential growth formula.

Here is the situation:

> ➢ This is an XY type graph, so you may want positions in between the observed values.

> ➢ Inserts in a graph are actually a new series of values, but you have to create the corresponding table of coordinates on your own. All its values can be found easily because there is an exponential formula behind some coordinates.

> ➢ To insert the new lines, you can either use the Add Data menu option or go to the Source Data and add a new series.

> ➢ These are the corresponding coordinates needed for one insert:
> > 0, 10000
> >
> > 5, 10000
> >
> > 5, 0

Figure - 52

Each insert requires three sets of two coordinates. This graph was created by using an exponential growth formula.

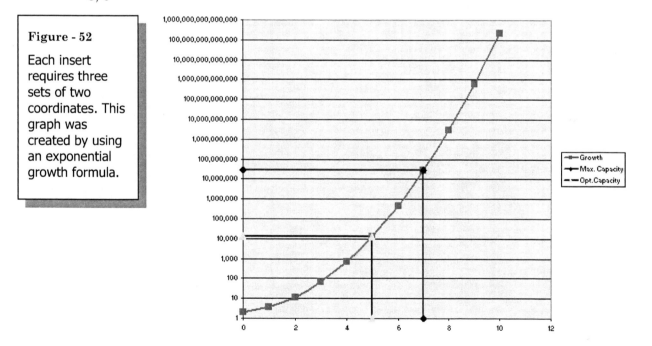

Here are the steps to take:

1. Type the coordinates shown in Table - 24 somewhere near your table.
2. Add them as a new series by using the Source Data option of the Chart menu.
3. Change the chart type by choosing XY, Subtype: Straight Lines.

Table - 24		
Type these sets of coordinates somewhere on your spreadsheet.		

0	10000 (formula)
5	10000 (formula)
5	0

Inserts Based on Nearest Observations

In the example shown in Figure - 52, we either based the curve on a formula or we were able to derive a formula from observations. You can use that same formula for the interpolated values.

But this trick doesn't help you when you don't know the equation behind the points found in your research. In a situation like this, you need to find a point that is located on a straight line between the two closest measurements. To find this point, you could use regular math (with proportional triangles) – or just apply Excel's *TREND* function, instead. Figure - 53 shows an example of this procedure.

Figure - 53
This sigmoid curve to the left is based on some observations. The insert is the result of interpolation by using the Trend function.

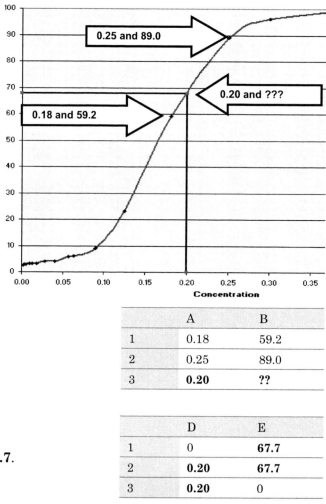

Let's assume that the curve to the right is based on observations, but you would like to interpolate what the absorption % is for a concentration of **0.20** (which you did not measure).

So you have the coordinates for two measurements, but you wonder about the second coordinate for concentration 0.20.

So, what is the second coordinate for 0.20?

	A	B
1	0.18	59.2
2	0.25	89.0
3	0.20	??

You can find it easily with the TREND function:

=TREND (B1:B2 , A1:A2 , A2)

The TREND function returns the answer: **67.7**.

	D	E
1	0	67.7
2	0.20	67.7
3	0.20	0

Implement the new coordinates somewhere on your spreadsheet, add them to the graph, and change the curve to a straight line type.

Inserts for Quality Control

Inserts can also have another purpose: demarcating the boundaries for quality control.

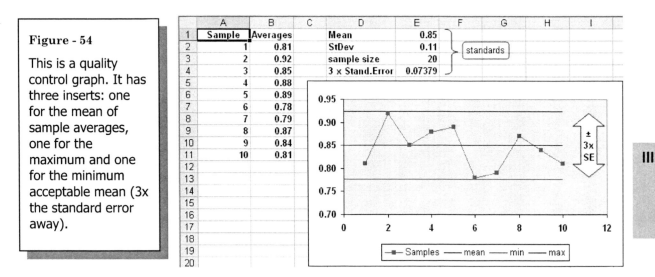

Figure - 54

This is a quality control graph. It has three inserts: one for the mean of sample averages, one for the maximum and one for the minimum acceptable mean (3x the standard error away).

Say you want to set the minimum and maximum boundaries at 3x the Standard Deviation (see Table - 25). You will need three horizontal lines – one for the mean at 0.85, one for the minimum at about 0.78, and one for the maximum at about 9.2.

Table - 25

This table holds two sets of coordinates for the mean, two sets for the minimum, and two sets for the maximum.

Mean	0	0.85
	10	0.85
Minimum	0	0.77621
	10	0.77621
Maximum	0	0.92379
	10	0.92379

It is obvious that somewhere on the sheet – hidden perhaps with a white font or behind the graph – you must create three series of coordinates. This time, each series needs only two sets of coordinates.

Adding Special Effects

Sometimes you may want to mark specific data in a graph – which is something like *Conditional Formatting*. Let's say you want to highlight the columns for pH>7 (see Figure - 55). The secret is to add a new series of values to the table (column C). This series is based on a certain condition:

=IF(pH>7, pH, NA())

 Note:

The function NA() creates a null value, which is different from zero or empty in that it will not show in a graph.

The first series of values (column B) is complete, but the second series (column C) displays only those few columns with a pH>7.

Because they show up next to each other, you must set the overlap between both series to 100%: R-Click on the series / *Format / Options / Overlap: 100.*

Figure - 55

A graph that highlights certain observations by using two series of values instead of one.

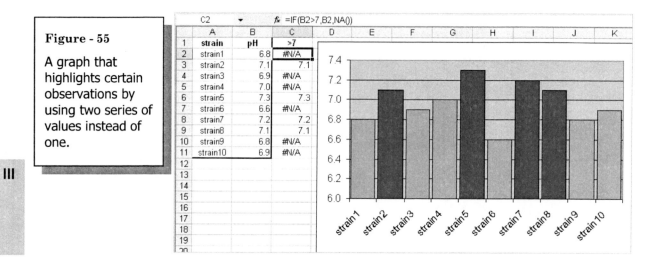

Sometimes a lot of work is required to get the look you want. Take a look at Figure - 56.

Figure - 56

Measurements are displayed with min, median, max, 25%, and 75% percentile per plate.

	A	B	C	D	E	F	G	H	I	J	K
1	Plate ID	1 hour	2 hours	3 hours			Min	25%	Median	75%	Max
2	8877p58a	37.7	22.7	10.7		8877p58a	9.5	10.9	23.0	36.4	39.3
3		38.7	23.0	10.5		8877p58b	9.2	10.1	22.7	33.5	37.5
4		39.3	23.0	10.9		8696p08a	11.2	12.7	26.7	40.1	46.4
5		35.9	22.9	9.5		8696p08b	11.4	12.9	26.5	39.0	42.9
6	8877p58b	37.5	22.7	10.1							
7		35.9	22.9	9.2			series1	series2	series3	series4	series5
8		33.2	22.6	9.9		8877p58a	9.5	1.4	12.1	13.4	3.0
9		34.3	20.7	9.9		8877p58b	9.2	0.9	12.6	10.8	4.0
10	8696p08a	46.4	29.1	12.8		8696p08a	11.2	1.5	14.1	13.4	6.3
11		41.3	26.9	11.7		8696p08b	11.4	1.5	13.6	12.5	3.9
12		42.3	26.5	12.2							
13		39.7	25.0	11.2							
14	8696p08b	42.9	27.5	13.1							
15		40.1	26.8	12.1							
16		41.0	26.1	12.3							
17		38.6	24.8	11.4							

The graph in Figure - 56 shows the median of measurements per plate, with the 25% percentile on both sides, plus the minimum and maximum measurement. All of this information was taken from the table to the left (columns A–D) by using calculations in the table on the top right (columns F–K; rows 1–5).

In order to transform this information into a *stacked bar* chart, we need one more table of calculations in between – which is the lower table to the right in Figure - 56 (columns F–K; rows 7–10). This table calculates the length of each section of each bar.

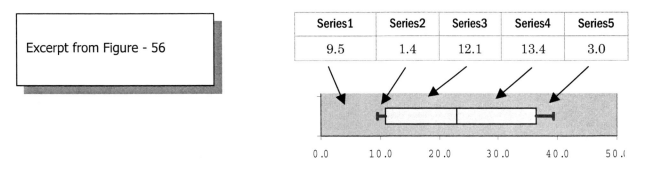

Excerpt from Figure - 56

Series1	Series2	Series3	Series4	Series5
9.5	1.4	12.1	13.4	3.0

Now we have to work on each series individually:

1. Series1: Set Border + Area to None.

2. Series2: The same as Series1, but add a minus Y-error bar of 100%.

3. Series3: Click OK.

4. Series4: Set color identical to Series3.

5. Series5: The same as Series1, but add a minus Y-error bar of 100%.

The only problem left is that the right-most Y-error bar is now reversed. We can solve this by taking the Y-error bar out of Series5 and adding one instead to Series4: a "custom plus" Y-error bar based on the values of Series5.

Working with Dynamic Ranges

What if you keep adding data at the bottom of your table? The graph will not update unless you use a dynamic reference: a range name based on the OFFSET function.

When you click on a specific Series in the graph, the formula bar shows its formula:

=SERIES(label, **categories, values,** order)

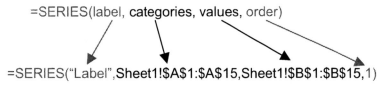

=SERIES("Label",Sheet1!$A$1:$A$15,Sheet1!$B$1:$B$15,1)

You could replace both categories and values with a dynamic range names by selecting *Insert / Name / Define* (see Naming Cells on page 6). Base both names on the OFFSET function.

=OFFSET(Start Cell, Offset Start Row, Offset Start Col, **Rows,** Cols)

Use the COUNTA function to count all category rows (A:A) and/or value rows (B:B).

=OFFSET (A1, 0, 0, **COUNTA(A:A)**)

Replace the cell addresses in the SERIES formula with the new names, and Excel will automatically replace the sheet names with book names when you hit Enter.

=SERIES("Label",Book1!**Range1**,Book1!**Range2**,1)

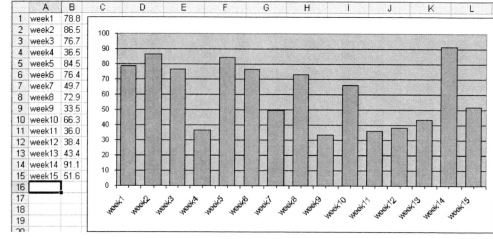

Figure - 57

This graph automatically expands when more weeks are added to the end of the table.

Another example: The graph shown in Figure - 58 has two cells in which you can set the lower and upper boundary of the graph. The steps are the same as before:

1. Create two dynamic Range Names: Weeks and Temperatures

2. Replace the cell references in the graph's Series function with these names.

3. Use these two settings for the Range Names:

> =OFFSET(Start Cell, **Offset Start Row**, Offset Start Col, **Rows**, Cols)

➤ For Weeks:

> =OFFSET(Sheet1!$A$1, Sheet1!$E$1-1, 0, Sheet1!$E$2- Sheet1!$E$1+1)

➤ For Temperatures:

> =OFFSET(Sheet1!$B$1, Sheet1!$E$1-1, 0, Sheet1!$E$2- Sheet1!$E$1+1)

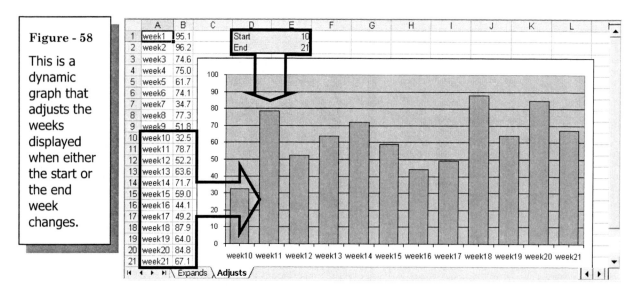

Figure - 58

This is a dynamic graph that adjusts the weeks displayed when either the start or the end week changes.

Exercise 25.

1. The curve of a falling ball:
   in A1: t (secs)
   in A2:A8: 0 through 6
   in B1: s (ft)
   in B2: 0
   in B3: 16

2. Formula in B4, etc:
   s = 16 * t2

3. Create a graph from these figures. Which type?

4. Add an insert for the distance at 4.5 seconds. The coordinates for the intersection are 4.5 and 648.

5. Adjust the graph so it looks like Figure - 59.

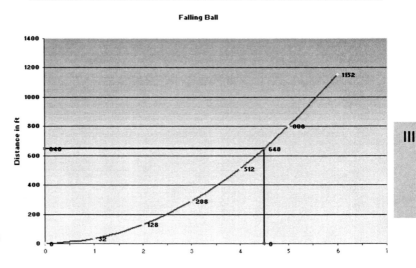

Figure - 59

The curve plots the distance a falling ball traveled during different time intervals.

III

Exercise 26.

1. Use the graph from Exercise 21. (See page 48.)

2. Create two inserts, one for 5% and one for 95%.

Exercise 27.

1. Use the table from Exercise 1. (See page 12.) Create an XY chart: Place the pH from column C on the X-axis, and the % of [AH] on the Y-axis.

2. Create an insert where the buffer works best: 50% and pH 4.7.

3. Fix the scales and make the X-axis more detailed (see Figure - 60).

Figure - 60

The buffer effect of a salt and its acid, with the optimal buffering effect at pH 4.7

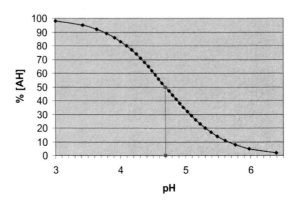

III

Chapter IV: Regression Analysis

Regression Analysis can be done either mathematically or graphically:

- ➢ Graphically with XY charts
- ➢ Mathematically with functions such as SLOPE, INTERCEPT, RSQ, and TREND

Mono-factorial and Linear

Mono-factorial linear regression assumes a linear relationship between two factors: a <u>dependent</u> factor Y and an <u>independent</u> factor X. You yourself decide which one of the two you want to declare the dependent factor, which you then derive from the independent factor by using a linear equation.

Figure - 61

A summary of the Least Squares Method

In a <u>mathematical</u> approach, this relationship can be described by the following linear equation:

$$Y = a_1 X + a_0$$

where a_1 is called the *slope* and a_0 is called the *intercept*.

This equation, which allows you to calculate Y (dependent) based on X (independent), is based on the *least squares method* (Figure - 61).

In a graphical approach, you can add regression lines (Excel calls them *trend lines*) to each series of values in the XY graph – including the above equations.

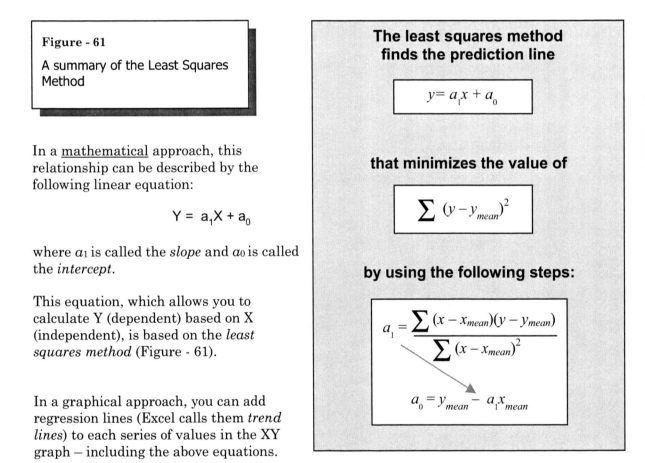

The least squares method finds the prediction line

$$y = a_1 x + a_0$$

that minimizes the value of

$$\sum (y - y_{mean})^2$$

by using the following steps:

$$a_1 = \frac{\sum (x - x_{mean})(y - y_{mean})}{\sum (x - x_{mean})^2}$$

$$a_0 = y_{mean} - a_1 x_{mean}$$

IV

The measured values are actually scattered around the regression line. The "measure of scatter" is also called *R-squared value* (RSQ). The closer this value comes to 1, the more accurate the prediction.

Figure - 62

Two simple linear regression lines

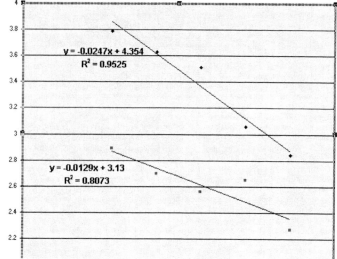

How can you add regression (or trend) lines like those in Figure - 62?

1. R-Click on a specific series of values.
2. Choose *Add Trendline.*
3. On the Type tab, choose your type.
4. On the Options tab, check ☑ Display equation and ☑ Display R-squared

In addition to the regression line for Y based on X, you could also calculate the opposite: the regression line for X based on Y. The smaller the angle between those two lines, the better the correlation. The *correlation coefficient* can range between −1 and 1. A correlation of ±1 stands for an angle of 0°; a correlation of 0 indicates an angle of 90° (which means no correlation at all).

Figure - 63 Derivation of Pearson's correlation coefficient

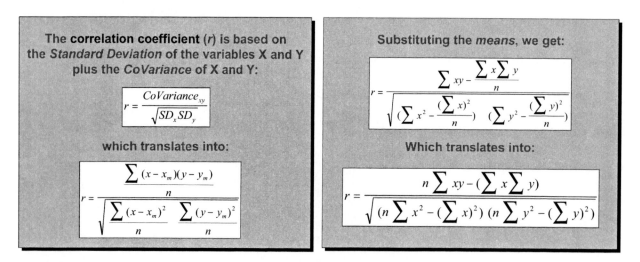

Earlier, we talked about the RSQ-value. This value is actually the squared correlation value, so RSQ is always positive (between 0 and 1).

To calculate *correlation coefficients*, you must use:

  🧪 CORREL for populations

  🧪 PEARSON for samples

Thanks to linear regression lines, we are able to calculate Y-values for specific X-values (even as interpolation or extrapolation). This can be done in at least two ways:

> Applying the formula $Y = a_1 X + a_0$, after using the SLOPE (a_1) and INTERCEPT (a_0) functions

> Using the TREND function

The TREND function, which is based on the <u>observed</u> X and Y values, calculates the <u>expected</u> Y values according to a linear regression line. You can also base calculations on <u>un</u>-observed (interpolated or extrapolated) X values. To do this, you need to add those values at the end of the list and create a second TREND calculation (do not do this in one single step!) where you can use the new, unobserved values as well.

TREND() is an <u>array</u> function (see Multiple-cell arrays on page 75). To use it, you need to:

1. Select multiple cells.
2. Assign arguments.
3. Hit Ctrl+Shift+Enter.

IV

Figure - 64

The TREND function can be used to calculate predicted values (based on linear regression) as well as interpolated values.

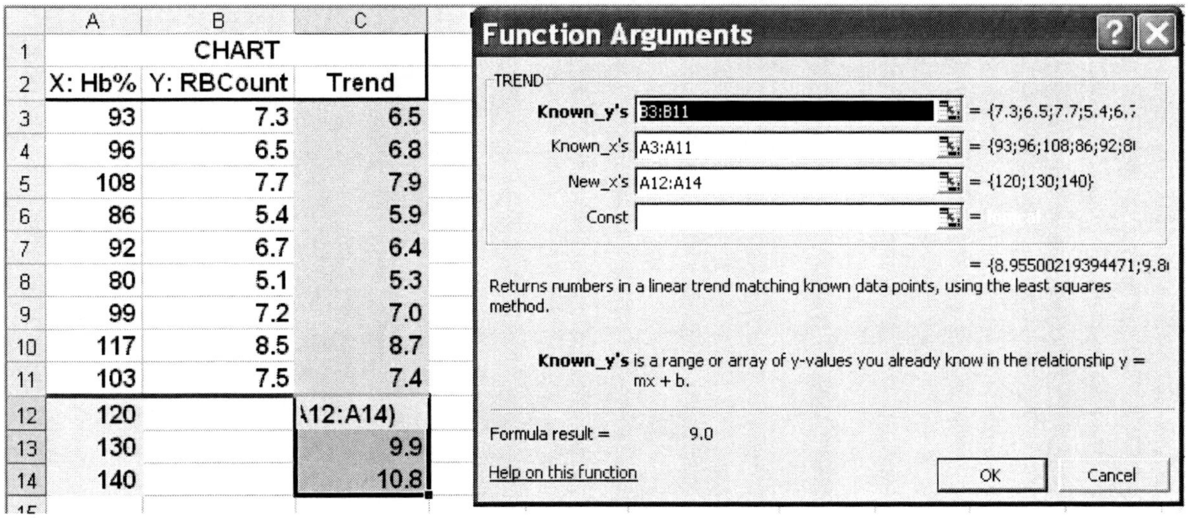

In the example of Figure - 64, the TREND function was used in two separate steps:

1. First in C3:C11: for observed Y's (B3:B11), observed X's (A3:A11)

2. Next in C12:C14: same setting as before, but this time adding <u>new</u> X's (A12:A14)

⚛ **Exercise 28.**

1. Create Table - 26 on a spreadsheet.
2. Consider Hb% to be the independent factor (X).
3. Calculate slope, intercept, and R-squared value.
4. Create a third column to predict RBCount based on Hb% (use slope and intercept).
5. Create a fourth column for the scatter (or residuals) between observed and expected values.
6. What should be the total of column 4?
7. Plot the first two columns in an XY chart.
8. Add a regression line, including its formula and R-squared value.

Table - 26

Relationship between % hemoglobin and the red blood cell count

X: Hb%	Y: RBCount
93	7.3
96	6.5
108	7.7
86	5.4
92	6.7
80	5.1
96	7.0
117	8.5
103	7.5

IV

⚛ **Exercise 29.**

1. Copy the first two columns of Exercise 28.
2. Create a third column to predict RBCount by using the TREND function
3. Plot all three columns in an XY chart.
4. At the bottom of the first column, add three extrapolated Hb% values: 120, 125, 130.
5. Use the TREND function again to predict RBCount.
6. Display those new values also in the graph.

Curve Fitting

When creating linear regressions, we construct a line that best fits the measured values. A "best fit" means that deviations above and below the line cancel each other out.

Theoretically, we can always construct a straight line that evens out aberrations, but this doesn't mean that a straight line is necessarily the best predictor. In other words, the regression may be *non-linear* – or there may be no reliable regression at all. To tackle this problem we need something that is called *curve fitting*.

You can go about this problem using trial and error. Just try different types of regression: logarithmic, exponential, or polynomial-to-the-power-of-2, etc. With each trial, check whether R-squared has come closer to 1 (R-Click on the trend line / *Format Trendline* / select the *Options tab* / check ☑ *Display equation* and ☑ *RSQ*).

OR you can create a new XY chart for the *scatter* values (usually called *residuals*). The pattern behind this chart may give you a clue as to what type of regression you are dealing with. If dots are equally distributed above and below the zero-line, then you probably have a strong case for linear regression.

Figure - 65

The curve to the left shows observed values plus a regression line with predicted values. The curve to the right shows the pattern of the residuals.

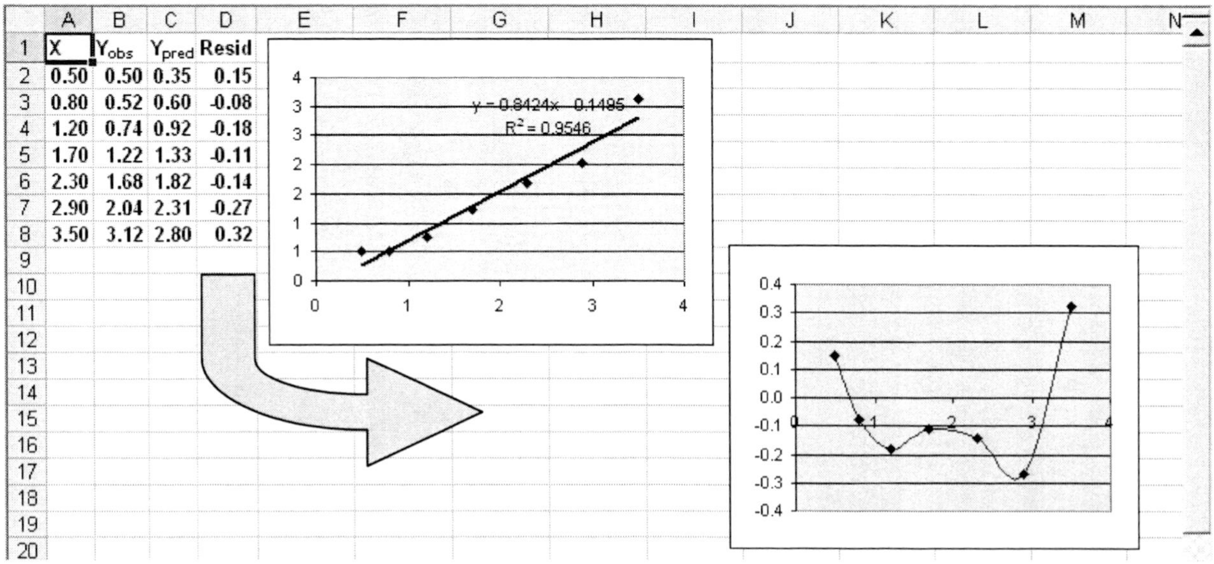

	A	B	C	D
1	X	Y_{obs}	Y_{pred}	**Resid**
2	0.50	0.50	0.35	0.15
3	0.80	0.52	0.60	-0.08
4	1.20	0.74	0.92	-0.18
5	1.70	1.22	1.33	-0.11
6	2.30	1.68	1.82	-0.14
7	2.90	2.04	2.31	-0.27
8	3.50	3.12	2.80	0.32

$y = 0.8424x - 0.1495$
$R^2 = 0.9546$

In the situation of Figure - 65, a linear regression line looks OK until we plot the residuals in a second graph. Since this second curve resembles a parabola, we know that the first regression line should be of the second power type. If you try this type, the RSQ value would actually go up from .95 to .98. You may want to try some more options (see Table - 27).

Table - 27

Formulas for several regression lines

Linear	$y = a_1x + a_0$
Parabola	$y = a_2x^2 + a_1x + a_0$
Cubic Curve	$y = a_3x^3 + a_2x^2 + a_1x + a_0$
*n*th Degree Curve	$y = a_nx^n + \ldots + a_1x + a_0$

Exercise 30.

1. Use the graph from Exercise 28. (See page 63.) See whether non-linear alternatives create a better fit.

IV

![atom icon] **Exercise 31.**

1. Start a new sheet.

2. Type in the cells A1:A20 this formula: =RAND()*10

3. Place in the cells B1:B20: =A1+RANDBETWEEN(−1,1)

4. Create an XY graph from these figures.

5. Add a linear regression line, including its formula plus RSQ value.

6. Test which type fits best. Press F9 to recalculate the random values.

Figure - 66

Linear regression line for two sets of random numbers. The first set is between 0 and 10. The second set is based on the parallel number in the other set, plus or minus 10%.

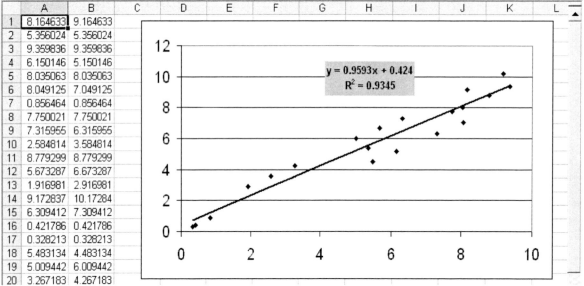

	A	B
1	8.164633	9.164633
2	5.356024	5.356024
3	9.359836	9.359836
4	6.150146	5.150146
5	8.035063	8.035063
6	8.049125	7.049125
7	0.856464	0.856464
8	7.750021	7.750021
9	7.315955	6.315955
10	2.584814	3.584814
11	8.779299	8.779299
12	5.673287	6.673287
13	1.916981	2.916981
14	9.172837	10.17284
15	6.309412	7.309412
16	0.421786	0.421786
17	0.328213	0.328213
18	5.483134	4.483134
19	5.009442	6.009442
20	3.267183	4.267183

$y = 0.9593x + 0.424$
$R^2 = 0.9345$

Multiple Regression

In simple linear regressions, we assume that only one factor impacts the dependent factor. But the real world is not that simple. Usually, other factors come into play. Factor Y may be dependent on factor X_1, but also on factor X_2, and so forth.

This is called *multi-factorial* or *multiple regression*. When curve fitting remains unsatisfactory, you may want to consider the impact of additional factors – something like this:

$$Y = a_n X_n + \dots + a_2 X_2 + a_1 X_1 + a_0$$

To calculate multiple slopes, we need an *array* function called LINEST. It returns a linear regression. This function also works on *mono-factorial* cases, but its use is mandatory for multi-factorial situations. Array functions require that you select multiple cells and that you accept the function with Ctrl+Shift+Enter rather than with just Enter (see also Array Formulas on page 74).

To use the LINEST() array function:

1. Select several cells.
2. Press Ctrl+Shift+Enter.

The function returns the slopes in reversed order, with the intercept displayed at the end.

=LINEST(array1, array2, true, true)

LINEST has two optional arguments:

> ➢ The third argument, when set to true, also calculates the intercept (otherwise, it's set to 0).

> ➢ The fourth argument of LINEST determines whether you want only the slopes and intercept (false) to be returned, or also some additional statistics (true), such as Standard Errors, and so forth. If you want to know what these additional statistics are, and in which order they appear, consult Help on LINEST (see Table - 28).

Usually, it is wise to calculate the correlation between Y and the other factors before you use LINEST. If the correlation is low for a specific independent factor, you probably will not use that particular factor in the multiple regression formula.

 Note:

You have to select all the cells you want to be filled <u>before</u> you apply LINEST.

Table - 28 The order of regression statistics returned by LINEST if fourth argument is set to True.	a_n	a_{n-1}	...	a_2	a_1	a_0
	SE a_n	SE a_{n-1}	...	SE a_2	SE a_1	SE a_0
	R^2	SE y				
	F	df				
	$SS_{regression}$	$SS_{residuals}$				

Table - 29

List of Excel's statistical functions

Function	Action
AVEDEV	Returns the average of the absolute deviations of data points from their mean
AVERAGE	Returns the average of its arguments
AVERAGEA	Returns the average of its arguments, including numbers, text, and logical values
BETADIST	Returns the cumulative beta probability density function
BETAINV	Returns the inverse of the cumulative beta probability density function
BINOMDIST	Returns the individual term binomial distribution probability
CHIDIST	Returns the one-tailed probability of the chi-squared distribution
CHIINV	Returns the inverse of the one-tailed probability of the chi-squared distribution
CHITEST	Returns the test for independence
CONFIDENCE	Returns the confidence interval for a population mean
CORREL	Returns the correlation coefficient between two data sets
COUNT	Counts how many numbers are in the list of arguments
COUNTA	Counts how many values are in the list of arguments
COVAR	Returns covariance, the average of the products of paired deviations
CRITBINOM	Returns the smallest value for which the cumulative binomial distribution is less than or equal to a criterion value
DEVSQ	Returns the sum of squares of deviations
EXPONDIST	Returns the exponential distribution
FDIST	Returns the F probability distribution
FINV	Returns the inverse of the F probability distribution
FISHER	Returns the Fisher transformation
FISHERINV	Returns the inverse of the Fisher transformation
FORECAST	Returns a value along a linear trend
FREQUENCY	Returns a frequency distribution as a vertical array
FTEST	Returns theResult of an F-test
GAMMADIST	Returns the gamma distribution
GAMMAINV	Returns the inverse of the gamma cumulative distribution
GAMMALN	Returns the natural logarithm of the gamma function, $\Gamma(x)$
GEOMEAN	Returns the geometric mean
GROWTH	Returns values along an exponential trend
HARMEAN	Returns the harmonic mean
HYPGEOMDIST	Returns the hypergeometric distribution
INTERCEPT	Returns the intercept of the linearRegression line
KURT	Returns the kurtosis of a data set
LARGE	Returns the k-th largest value in a data set
LINEST	Returns the parameters of a linear trend
LOGEST	Returns the parameters of an exponential trend

IV

Function	Action
LOGINV	Returns the inverse of the lognormal distribution
LOGNORMDIST	Returns the cumulative lognormal distribution
MAX	Returns the maximum value in a list of arguments
MAXA	Returns the maximum value in a list of arguments, including numbers, text, and logical values
MEDIAN	Returns the median of the given numbers
MIN	Returns the minimum value in a list of arguments
MINA	Returns the smallest value in a list of arguments, including numbers, text, and logical values
MODE	Returns the most common value in a data set
NEGBINOMDIST	Returns the negative binomial distribution
NORMDIST	Returns the normal cumulative distribution
NORMINV	Returns the inverse of the normal cumulative distribution
NORMSDIST	Returns the standard normal cumulative distribution
NORMSINV	Returns the inverse of the standard normal cumulative distribution
PEARSON	Returns the Pearson product moment correlation coefficient
PERCENTILE	Returns the k-th percentile of values in aRange
PERCENTRANK	Returns the percentageRank of a value in a data set
PERMUT	Returns the number of permutations for a given number of objects
POISSON	Returns the Poisson distribution
PROB	Returns the probability that values in aRange are between two limits
QUARTILE	Returns the quartile of a data set
RANK	Returns theRank of a number in a list of numbers
RSQ	Returns the square of the Pearson product moment correlation coefficient
SKEW	Returns the skewness of a distribution
SLOPE	Returns the slope of the linearRegression line
SMALL	Returns the k-th smallest value in a data set
STANDARDIZE	Returns a normalized value
STDEV	Estimates standard deviation based on a sample
STDEVA	Estimates standard deviation based on a sample, including numbers, text, and logical values
STDEVP	Calculates standard deviation based on the entire population
STDEVPA	Calculates standard deviation based on the entire population, including numbers, text, and logical values
STEYX	Returns the standard error of the predicted y-value for each x in theRegression
TDIST	Returns the Student's t-distribution
TINV	Returns the inverse of the Student's t-distribution
TREND	Returns values along a linear trend
TRIMMEAN	Returns the mean of the interior of a data set
TTEST	Returns the probability associated with a Student's t-test
VAR	Estimates variance based on a sample

IV

Function	Action
VARA	Estimates variance based on a sample, including numbers, text, and logical values
VARP	Calculates variance based on the entire population
VARPA	Calculates variance based on the entire population, including numbers, text, and logical values
WEIBULL	Returns the Weibull distribution
ZTEST	Returns the two-tailed P-value of a z-test

Exercise 32.

Use the values from Table - 30. We want to predict FVC based on age, height, and weight.

1. Calculate the correlations between FVC and each of those three factors.

2. Use LINEST to find the three slopes for each variable and the intercept (don't forget Ctrl+Shift+Enter).

3. Predict in column 5 what FVC should be, based on this regression line.

Table - 30

Data for Age, Height, Weight, and Forced Vital Capacity

Age	Height	Weight	FVC
60	171.3	48.5	2.84
50	167.6	55.8	3.06
40	170.0	57.1	3.51
30	170.4	60.9	3.63
20	171.0	60.6	3.79

Sometimes a Radar type of graph can help you to visualize some of this information. Be aware, though, that the graph uses categories at the end points (not values).

Figure - 67

A Radar graph showing how FVC is correlated with Age, Height, and Weight

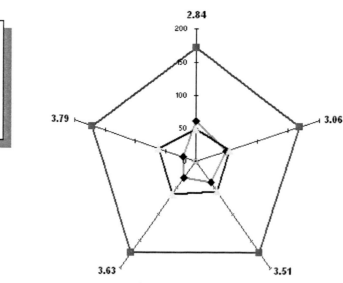

Chapter V: Complex Functions

Functions in Excel may have 0 to n *arguments*:

> ➤ NA(), RAND()(), and NOW() have <u>no</u> arguments
>
> ➤ STANDARDIZE(Z) requires <u>one</u> argument
>
> ➤ COUNTIF(range, condition) requires <u>two</u> arguments
>
> ➤ IF(test, if-true, if-false) holds <u>three</u> arguments; if the last two are not provided, they return either true or false
>
> ➤ NORMDIST(X, mean, stdev, cumulative) requires four arguments

All functions return a value, which can be of several types (see Table - 31.):

Table - 31

Types of values a function can return

Type	Size	Remarks	Range
Integer	2 bytes		±3,2767
Long	4 bytes		±2,147,483,647
Single	4 bytes	Precision up to 7 decimals/digits	±1.4E-50 – 3.4E43
Double	8 bytes	Precision up to 15 decimals/digits	±4.9E-337 – 1.7E321
Date	8 bytes		1/1/100 – 12/31/9999
Boolean	2 bytes		1 (on) and 0 (off)
String			Variable length
Variant	16 bytes		Any of the above

- *Integer* (no decimals, up to 32,000)
- *Long* (no decimals, up to 2,1 billion)
- *Single* (precision seven digits and/or decimals)
- *Double* (precision up to 15 digits and/or decimals)
- *Date* (number)
- *Boolean* (yes/no)
- *String* (text or formatted numbers)

Of course, you can always just <u>type</u> a function – but then you need to remember to start with an equal sign, to put in opening and closing parenthesis after the function name, and to use commas to separate arguments. Alternatively, you can use the f_x <u>button</u> on your toolbar or formula bar – then you only need to type the arguments. Excel puts all the rest in for you, including parentheses and commas.

Table - 32

A few examples of functions and their return types

Function	Return Type
AND()	*Boolean*
INT()	*Integer*
NOW()	*Date*
SQRT()	*Double*
UPPER()	*String* of capitalized text

Fancy Functions

Using IF

IF() is a very powerful and universal function. The IF function makes decisions for you according to your own rules, as expressed in its arguments.

The following is a simple example:

$$IF(t_{actual} < t_{critical}, \text{"Random", "Significant"})$$

Sometimes you want more than two choices. That's where *nested* IF-functions come in. Say you want three choices: random, significant, and highly significant:

$$IF(t_{actual} < t_{95\%}, \text{"Random"}, IF(t_{actual} < t_{97.5\%}, \text{"Significant", "Highly Significant"}))$$

You can have up to seven nested IF-functions, for a total of eight IF functions.

 Note:

IF() returns a Boolean number if you don't specify the "if-true" and "if-false" arguments.

Using VLOOKUP and MATCH

If you want more than three or four choices, your best bet is to create a small table of choices and use the VLOOKUP or HLOOKUP function:

🍶 VLOOKUP looks for a specific value in the first column of a table(**V**ertical)

🍶 HLOOKUP searches in the first row of a table(**H**orizontal)

$$=VLOOKUP(\text{what, table, column, match})$$

 Note:

If the match argument is False, the function searches for an exact match; otherwise, it searches for the closest previous match in ascending order. Choose True for a column of ascending values with intervals.

Figure - 68

Using functions to find an analyst's Group and Testing status in a listing of analysts to the right

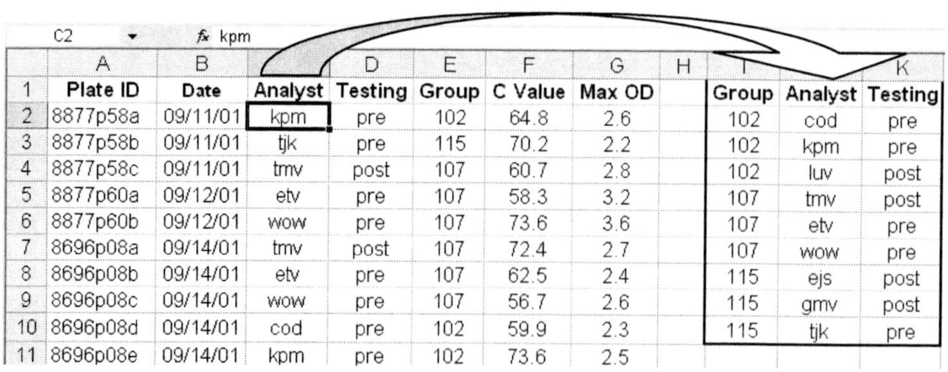

	C2		f_x kpm							
	A	B	C	D	E	F	G	H	I	J	K
1	Plate ID	Date	Analyst	Testing	Group	C Value	Max OD		Group	Analyst	Testing
2	8877p58a	09/11/01	kpm	pre	102	64.8	2.6		102	cod	pre
3	8877p58b	09/11/01	tjk	pre	115	70.2	2.2		102	kpm	pre
4	8877p58c	09/11/01	tmv	post	107	60.7	2.8		102	luv	post
5	8877p60a	09/12/01	etv	pre	107	58.3	3.2		107	tmv	post
6	8877p60b	09/12/01	wow	pre	107	73.6	3.6		107	etv	pre
7	8696p08a	09/14/01	tmv	post	107	72.4	2.7		107	wow	pre
8	8696p08b	09/14/01	etv	pre	107	62.5	2.4		115	ejs	post
9	8696p08c	09/14/01	wow	pre	107	56.7	2.6		115	gmv	post
10	8696p08d	09/14/01	cod	pre	102	59.9	2.3		115	tjk	pre
11	8696p08e	09/14/01	kpm	pre	102	73.6	2.5				

Take a look at Figure - 68. Let's say that we want cell D2 to have the Testing information for Analyst kpm based on data in the table to the right. Since VLOOKUP searches in the first column and the table is in columns J and K, it will find its answer in the second column (K). So, the formula in D2 is:

=VLOOKUP(C2, $J$2:$K$10, 2, True)

At this point, we know that the answer is to be found in column 2 of the table. But there is also a function that finds out exactly what the number of that column (or row) is. This function is called MATCH().

When you need to find out in which row or column a certain number or word is located, use the MATCH function. It returns the (relative) position of a row or column in a specific range. If the range starts in A1, its position 1 is actually row 1 or column 1.

=MATCH(*what, range, match-type*)

 Note:

If the match-type argument is zero, the function searches for an exact match; if the type is one, it searches for the previous match (in ascending order); if the type is two, it searches for the next match (in descending order).

Table - 33

If we use the MATCH function in the data to the left, we would find the answers shown on the right.

A1	B1	C1	D1
10	20	30	40

MATCH(20, A1:D1, 0) returns 2 (for position 2)

MATCH (**25**, A1:D1, 0) returns #NA (no exact match found)

MATCH (25, A1:D1, **1**) returns 2 (previous in *asc*)

MATCH (25, A1:D1, **–1**) returns #NA (range not descending)

We could also have used MATCH <u>inside</u> VLOOKUP as a "nested" function:

=VLOOKUP (C2, $J$2:$K$10, **2**, True)

Instead of using the number 2, try using MATCH:

=VLOOKUP (..., ..., **MATCH($D$1, $J$1:$K$1, 0)**, True)

Using INDEX

Now we are ready to tackle a function that is more flexible than VLOOKUP – the INDEX function. Its advantage is that it can look up values in any table position (not just the first row or column), but its disadvantage is that it works with row and column numbers (but that's where MATCH comes in handy).

When using the INDEX function, make sure it is of the first type (returning <u>values</u>):

=INDEX(range, row#, col#)

| E2 | ▾ | | *fx* | =INDEX($I$1:$K$10,MATCH(C2,$J$1:$J$10,0),MATCH($E$1,$I$1:$K$1,0)) | | | | | | |

Figure - 69

The same table as that used in Figure - 67. In cell E2, we want to find the analyst's (C2) group by looking up information in the listing to the right.

	A	B	C	D	E	F	G	H	I	J	K
1	Plate ID	Date	Analyst	Testing	Group	C Value	Max OD		Group	Analyst	Testing
2	8877p58a	09/11/01	kpm	pre	102	64.8	2.6		102	cod	pre
3	8877p58b	09/11/01	tjk	pre	115	70.2	2.2		102	kpm	pre
4	8877p58c	09/11/01	tmv	post	107	60.7	2.8		102	luv	post
5	8877p60a	09/12/01	etv	pre	107	58.3	3.2		107	tmv	post
6	8877p60b	09/12/01	wow	pre	107	73.6	3.6		107	etv	pre
7	8696p08a	09/14/01	tmv	post	107	72.4	2.7		107	wow	pre
8	8696p08b	09/14/01	etv	pre	107	62.5	2.4		115	ejs	post
9	8696p08c	09/14/01	wow	pre	107	56.7	2.6		115	gmv	post
10	8696p08d	09/14/01	cod	pre	102	59.9	2.3		115	tjk	pre
11	8696p08e	09/14/01	kpm	pre	102	73.6	2.5				

Refer to cell E2 in Figure - 69. We want to find kpm's group (which is 102) by using the listing to the right. The INDEX function can do this for us (see Table - 34 for some options):

Table - 34

The INDEX function requires row and column numbers, which can be hard numbers or values returned by a MATCH function.

With row # + col #	=INDEX($I$1:$K$10, **3**, **1**)
MATCH for row #	=INDEX($I$1:$K$10, MATCH(C2,$J$1:$J$10,0), 1)
MATCH for row # MATCH for col #	=INDEX($I$1:$K$10, MATCH(C2,$J$1:$J$10,0), MATCH($E$1,$I$1:$K$1,0))

Make sure that the range used in INDEX starts at the same row or column as the range used in MATCH, because MATCH returns a <u>relative</u> row or column position. Obviously, you can replace range addresses with range names if you prefer to do so.

Table - 35

The order in which LINEST returns regression stats

a_n	a_0
SE a_n	SE a_0
R^2	SE y
F	df
$SS_{regression}$	$SS_{residuals}$

Needless to say, you can also use INDEX to get a specific return value from the multiple values returned by an *array* function such as LINEST (see Table - 35):

$$=INDEX(LINEST(y, x, True, True), \textbf{3}, \textbf{1})$$

In this case, LINEST would return the R^2 value of a linear regression line.

Exercise 33.

1. Use the Random Number Generator to create, in column A, 20 random numbers with a mean of 10 and a standard deviation of 0.5.

2. Calculate the actual mean and standard deviation.

3. In column B, calculate the absolute difference between each number and the mean.

4. In column C, use an IF-function to display ">.5x" if the number is more than half the stdev from the mean.

5. Enhance that formula for a more detailed specification: "" OR ">.5x" OR ">1x"

6. Sort the table by column A and check the extremes.

Exercise 34.

1. Find the closest downward Apparent Temperature for 92° F and 52% humidity in Table - 36A.

2. Use VLOOKUP and MATCH to find your answer.

3. Use HLOOKUP and MATCH to find your answer.

4. Use INDEX and 2x MATCH to find your answer.

Table - 36A		70	80	90	100
A table of Apparent Temperature (in F) for Air Temperature (first row in F) and Relative Humidity (first column in %).	0%	64	73	83	91
	50%	69	81	96	120
	70%	70	85	106	144

5. Place a formula in the Search Box of Table - 36B that finds the severity of any MPH wind setting by using one of the LOOKUP functions with a nested MATCH function.

6. Create a formula that finds the surge value for any MPH value by using the INDEX function and two nested MATCH functions.

Table - 36B

A table of Hurricane categories

Hurricanes

wind MPH	0	74	96	111	131	155
severity	none	weak	moderate	strong	very strong	devastating
storm surge	0 ft.	4 ft.	6 ft.	9 ft.	13 ft.	18 ft.

Search Box

wind MPH	55
severity	none
storm surge	0 ft.

Array Formulas

Array formulas are very special, powerful formulas: They use internal arrays for two different purposes:

1. To return <u>multiple</u> values stored in an array. In cases like these, you need to select multiple cells in order to display the values returned by the array.

2. To return a <u>single</u> value that was calculated from several sub-calculations stored in an array. Here you need to select a single cell to display the result.

Array formulas – whether they are single-cell or multiple-cell – must be finalized with Ctrl+Shift+Enter (not just Enter). You can never delete or change any part of the array (which is in fact a life-saver for your formulas). Only an entire array can be deleted; if you need to locate its borders, use *Edit / GoTo / Special / Current Array.*

Array functions are displayed in the formula bar with braces {...}. When you click in the bar, the braces disappear until you press Ctrl+Shift+Enter again.

Note: Do NOT <u>type</u> the braces! They come with Ctrl+Shift+Enter. Each time you click in the formula bar, you must use Ctrl+Shift+Enter again.

Multiple-cell arrays

LINEST is a multiple-cell type of array: It calculates multiple results (such as several slopes, an intercept, and a bunch of other statistics). Therefore, you need to select as many cells as necessary to display these results. The same holds for FREQUENCY, and other multiple-cell array functions.

Examples of multiple-cell type array functions include the following:

♨ TREND() – We used this array function in the Putting Inserts in Graphs section on page 53 and the Mono-factorial and Linear section on page 60.

♨ LINEST() – We used this array function in the Multiple Regression section on page 65.

♨ FREQUENCY() – We used this array function in the Using Normal Distribution section on page 14.

♨ TRANSPOSE() – Try this: Place entries in cells A1:A3 (three <u>vertical</u> cells). Select B1:D1 (three <u>horizontal</u> cells) and type: =TRANSPOSE(A1:A3). Then hit Ctrl+Shift+Enter, and you will get a transposed copy in B1:D1 from A1:A3.

If you want to see an array function "perform," highlight all or part of the function in the formula bar and then press F9 to make Excel calculate. You see the results displayed in the formula bar. Do not hit Enter now, for the results would replace the formula. Instead you must hit Esc to get the original formula back.

Exercise 35.

Let us create a "rotated" version of the table used in Exercise 34.

1. How many empty rows and columns should you select for your range?

2. Type in the formula bar: =TRANSPOSE(range) and set that range to your original table.

3. Accept this formula for all selected cells: Ctrl+Shift+Enter.

Exercise 36.

Use the random numbers from Exercise 33. (or Exercise 24.) (See page 74 or page 51.)

1. Create 13 bins with an interval of 0.25: from 8.50 up to 11.50. Make sure they are in a vertical column!

2. Select all the corresponding cells in the next column.

3. Use the FREQUENCY function and Ctrl+Shift+Enter.

4. Does this function update when the numbers change?

Single-cell arrays

Array functions also allow you to manipulate information from several cells with the help of temporary arrays. The end value is single, but is still based on array operations.

Let's say that you want the average of the RBCount for cases with an Hb% > 100 (see Exercise 28.):

Hb%	RBCount
93	7.3
96	6.5
108	7.7
86	5.4
92	6.7
80	5.1
96	7.0
117	8.5
103	7.5

$$=AVERAGE(IF (A2:A10>100,B2:B10))$$

Don't forget Ctrl+Shift+Enter!!!

The answer is 7.9, based on comparing an array holding true/false values for A2:A10 with an array holding RBC values from B2:B10.

Here are some basic rules for single-cell arrays:

- =SUM(IF(..., A1:A9) totals values in A1:A9 where the test is true

- =SUM(IF(A1:A9>..., 1, 0) actually counts values in A1:A9 if the test is true

- =SUM(IF((...) * (...), A1:A9) sums values when both conditions are true

- =SUM(IF((...) + (...), A1:A9) sums values if either condition is true

Each formula of Table - 37 was created in a single cell, finalized with Ctrl+Shift+Enter, and then copied downwards to the other cells.

Figure - 70

The table section to the right uses single-cell array formulas to find for each analyst (column I) a count, a mean, and a count for OD>2 based on the left section.

	A	B	C	D	E	F	G	H	I	J	K	L
1	Plate ID	Date	Analyst	Testing	Group	C Value	Max OD			Count	Mean C	OD>2
2	8877p58a	09/11/01	kpm	pre	102	64.8	2.6		cod	2	52.5	2
3	8877p58b	09/11/01	tjk	pre	115	70.2	2.2		ejs	3	56.9	2
4	8877p58c	09/11/01	tmv	post	107	60.7	2.8		etv	4	69.7	3
5	8877p60a	09/12/01	etv	pre	107	58.3	3.2		gmv	2	70.4	0
6	8877p60b	09/12/01	wow	pre	107	73.6	3.6		kpm	4	61.7	3
7	8696p08a	09/14/01	tmv	post	107	72.4	2.7		luv	3	58.2	3
8	8696p08b	09/14/01	etv	pre	107	62.5	2.4		tjk	3	58.3	1
9	8696p08c	09/14/01	wow	pre	107	56.7	2.6		tmv	4	65.7	3
10	8696p08d	09/14/01	cod	pre	102	59.9	2.3		wow	3	64.0	3
11	8696p08e	09/14/01	kpm	pre	102	73.6	2.5					
12	8696p08f	09/14/01	luv	post	102	63.3	2.4					
13	8877p63a	09/14/01	cod	pre	102	45.0	2.8					
14	8877p63b	09/14/01	kpm	pre	102	50.2	2.7					
15	8877p70c	09/18/01	gmv	post	115	57.1	1.4					
16	8877p70d	09/18/01	tjk	pre	115	39.8	1.1					
17	8877p71a	09/19/01	tmv	post	107	66.9	2.7					

You can highlight (parts of) the formula in the formula bar to see its performance after you hit F9. Then hit Esc, not Enter!

This trick may help you when an array formula doesn't work quite the way you expect it to.

Table - 37

Array formulas used in the right section of Figure - 70

J2:

=SUM(IF($C$2:$C$29=I2,1,0))

K2:

=AVERAGE(IF($C$2:$C$29=I2,$F$2:$F$29))

L2:

=SUM(IF(($C$2:$C$29=I2) * ($G$2:$G$29>2),1,0))

Exercise 37.

1. Use the numbers, bins, and frequencies from Exercise 36. Find the average for all numbers higher than 10.

2. Average the differences between each value and the mean in ONE formula (the result should be 0!).

3. How many bins have more than three cases?

4. Find the sum of all random numbers with a precision of two decimals. To do so, you could use an array function: =SUM(ROUND(..., 2))

Homemade Functions

There are times that Excel does not provide the specific function that you really need. No problem. Create that function yourself! You can do so in the *VBA Editor*. Just hit Alt+F11 to open the VBA Editor. Then, if necessary, select *Insert / Module*.

This is the skeleton of a function:

Function XXX(...) As ...

    XXX = ...

End Function

XXX	is the unique name of the function
(...)	allows for a number of arguments
As ...	specifies the type of return value (Table - 31)
= ...	specifies which calculation is performed

Let's create the following simple *user-defined* or *custom* functions:

> DateStamp
> TimeStamp
> CubicRoot
> AnyRoot
> StError

DateStamp returns today's date – but in a format that you choose.

1. Type in VBA: Function DateStamp() As Single
2. After you hit Enter, fill in the function between the first and last line: DateStamp = Date
3. Now use that new function in Excel by selecting an empty cell and clicking on f_x so that you can locate DateStamp in the list.
4. Go back to VBA and change As Single into As String.
5. Change DateStamp=Date into DateStamp=Format(Date, "ddd m/d/yy").
6. Go back to the cell and update the function with the F9 key.

TimeStamp returns the current time in hours, minutes, and seconds.

1. Type in VBA: Function TimeStamp() As String
2. Type: TimeStamp = Now() – Date (Now() returns date and time, which is a date with decimals, whereas in VBA, Date returns only the date (see Managing Dates on page 9).
3. On the next line, type: TimeStamp = Format(TimeStamp, "h:mm:ss")
4. Test the new function on an Excel sheet. Note that F9 will not update the time until you add the following new VBA code line: Application.Volatile. This is necessary because Now() is a volatile function.

CubeRoot calculates and returns the cube root of any number (Excel only offers a square-root function), but this time we need to specify the number of which we want the root (which is called a function's argument or parameter).

1. Type in VBA: Function CubeRoot(num As Double) As Double
2. On the next line, type: CubeRoot = num ^ (1 / 3)
3. Test this function on an Excel sheet.

AnyRoot is a function that returns any root of any number.

1. Type in VBA: Function AnyRoot(num As Double, root As Integer) As String
2. On next line, type: AnyRoot = num ^ (1 / root)
3. Test this function on an Excel sheet.

StError is another helpful function that Excel does not provide. It returns the standard error for the sampling distribution based on a sample's standard deviation and size.

1. Type in VBA: Function StError(sd As Double, size As Double) As Double
2. On next line, type: StError = sd / sqr(size)
   (FYI: VBA uses SQR, Excel uses SQRT)
   You could also use your own function: StError = sd / AnyRoot(size, 2)
3. Test this function on an Excel sheet.

Tip:

For more information on VBA, consult the interactive CD "Slide Your Way Through Excel VBA" from MrExcel, available through www.mrexcel.com or www.amazon.com.

Whenever you use a customized function like StError, you will see the following at the bottom of the function's dialog box (see Figure - 71):

StError(Dev,Size)
No help available.

V

Figure - 71

An example of how user-created functions automatically show up in the *Insert Function* dialog box

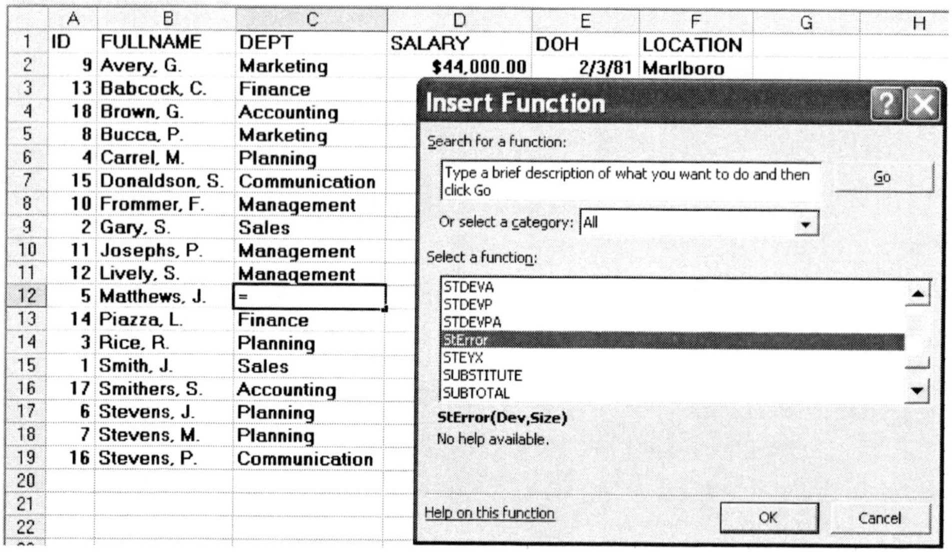

	A	B	C	D	E	F	G	H
1	ID	FULLNAME	DEPT	SALARY	DOH	LOCATION		
2	9	Avery, G.	Marketing	$44,000.00	2/3/81	Marlboro		
3	13	Babcock, C.	Finance					
4	18	Brown, G.	Accounting					
5	8	Bucca, P.	Marketing					
6	4	Carrel, M.	Planning					
7	15	Donaldson, S.	Communication					
8	10	Frommer, F.	Management					
9	2	Gary, S.	Sales					
10	11	Josephs, P.	Management					
11	12	Lively, S.	Management					
12	5	Matthews, J.	=					
13	14	Piazza, L.	Finance					
14	3	Rice, R.	Planning					
15	1	Smith, J.	Sales					
16	17	Smithers, S.	Accounting					
17	6	Stevens, J.	Planning					
18	7	Stevens, M.	Planning					
19	16	Stevens, P.	Communication					
20								
21								
22								

Insert Function

Search for a function:

Type a brief description of what you want to do and then click Go   Go

Or select a category: All

Select a function:

STDEVA
STDEVP
STDEVPA
StError
STEYX
SUBSTITUTE
SUBTOTAL

StError(Dev,Size)
No help available.

Help on this function   OK   Cancel

If you want to, you can add a short Help feature to the function. Here's how:

1. In Excel, select *Tools / Macro / Macros.*
2. In the name box, type: StError
3. Hit the Options button.
4. Type in a short description.

It is also possible to make one or more arguments *optional*, including the default setting. This means that users of your function do not have to specify the optional argument(s); if they don't, the argument will take its default setting. However, optional arguments must always be placed at the end of the arguments listing.

Let us apply this concept to two of the functions we have already created.

AnyRoot has two arguments at this moment: num and root. We could make the second argument optional and give it a default value of 2. If the user of your function does not specify the second argument, it will default to 2.

   1. Replace root As Integer with Optional root As Integer = 2.
       Now the first line reads:
       Function AnyRoot(num As Double, Optional root As Integer = 2) As Double

   2. Test the new setting.

TimeStamp has no arguments yet, but we could create an optional argument that determines whether the function updates or not.

   1. Create an argument: Optional fixed As Boolean = True

   2. Replace Application.Volatile with: If fixed = False Then Application.Volatile

   3. Test the new setting.

Figure - 72
The VBA code behind the five custom functions created in this chapter

```
Function DateStamp() As String
    DateStamp = Format(Date, "ddd m/d/yy")
End Function


Function TimeStamp(Optional fixed As Boolean = True) As String
    If fixed = False Then Application.Volatile
    TimeStamp = Format(Now() - Date, "h:mm:ss")
End Function


Function CubeRoot(num As Double) As Double
    CubeRoot = num ^ (1 / 3)
End Function


Function AnyRoot(num As Double, Optional root As Integer = 2) As Double
    AnyRoot = num ^ (1 / root)
End Function


Function StError(SD As Double, size As Double) As Double
    StError = SD / Sqr(size)
End Function
```

 Exercise 38.

   1. Create a new function that calculates the growth of a population based on an initial size, a rate, and a number of generations.

   2. How many arguments does this function require?

   3. What value type should the function return?

   4. Create and use the new function in a table with rates 2.0, 2.2, ... 3.0 and generations 10, 20, ... 50, but use an initial size of 2.

   5. How precise are the results?

6. Apply a description to the function.

7. Make the initial size argument optional with a default of 2 (but move it to the end of the list of arguments).

Solving Equations

Formulas re-calculate when you change the values they are based on. But what if you want to do the opposite: changing the results of those formulas – which is comparable to a what-if analysis?

There are two very different ways of going about this problem:

➤ Use the tools Excel provides to find specific solutions for your formulas or equations.

➤ Create a table that shows the results of your formulas while you keep your variables "under control" with *Controls.*

Excel Tools for solving equations

There are two tools that Excel provides for solving equations: *GoalSeek* and *Solver* (see Figure - 73).

GoalSeek is the simpler tool. You can set the result of a formula to a certain value and determine which value you want to change in order to obtain that result. Select a formula and go to: *Tools / GoalSeek.* There may be several solutions, but Solver seeks a solution starting at the current value (a "guess") but in the direction where the function moves closer to the target (see Figure - 74, where your goal is: X=0)).

Solver is the fancier tool. It does the same operations as GoalSeek, but, in addition, Solver finds the minimum and maximum settings and it allows you to set certain *constraints*. Also, you can vary more than one cell.

	GoalSeek	Solver
Target cell	Cell w/formula set to a value	Cell w/formula can be set to value/max/min
Changing	One value cell used in Target	>= Cell w/values or formulas
Constraints	–	On changing values or related formulas

Figure - 73

Overview of the differences between GoalSeek and Solver.

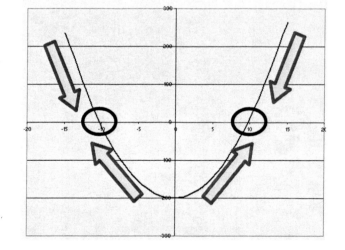

Figure - 74

GoalSeek and Solver seek in the direction where the function moves closer to the target value.

Go to *Tools / Solver*. If Solver hasn't been installed, do this: *Tools / Add-Ins / ☑ Solver*

You can influence the way Solver tries to find solutions by clicking on the Options button in the Solver menu screen (see Table - 38 on page 85 for a list of Options settings).

Let's use the following example: A population of five individuals (N0) has an intrinsic growth rate of 0.5 (r), but its maximum level is 1000 individuals (K). In the beginning, the actual growth rate (R) is equal to the intrinsic rate (r), producing an exponential increase in population size. But in time, the actual growth rate slows down until finally, at N=K, R comes down to zero. This produces a sigmoid curve described by the following exponential equation:

$$N' = \frac{K}{1 + \left(\dfrac{K - N_0}{N_0}\right) e^{-rt'}}$$

When used in Excel in cell D11 (see Figure - 75), the formula would look like this (see Table - 39 on page 88 for a list of Excel's Math and Trig functions):

=$D$8/(1+(($D$8-$D$10)/$D$10)*EXP(1)^(-$D$7*$D$9))

Figure - 75

The table to the left holds a series of variables that are used in the formula of cell D11. The graph to the right shows the sigmoid curve for population growth in the course of time. The insert in the graph depicts the setting as specified in the table to the left.

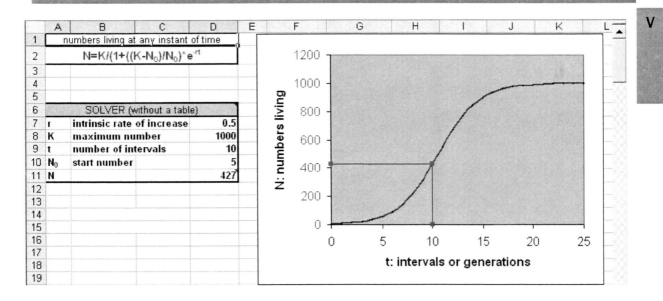

Refer to Figure - 75. To find out what *N* would be after 15 intervals (or generations), you can just type 15 in cell D9, and cell D11 will automatically update. Remember, D7:D10 holds real numbers, whereas D11 has a formula in it based on D7:D10. But can we ever find out after how many generations (*t*) the population reaches 800 individuals (N)?

Let's not go for trial-and-error. Instead, we can use either GoalSeek or Solver to find our answer. In either case, the solution will be 13 intervals!

Figure - 76

The left panel shows the use of GoalSeek. The right panel displays the settings for Solver.

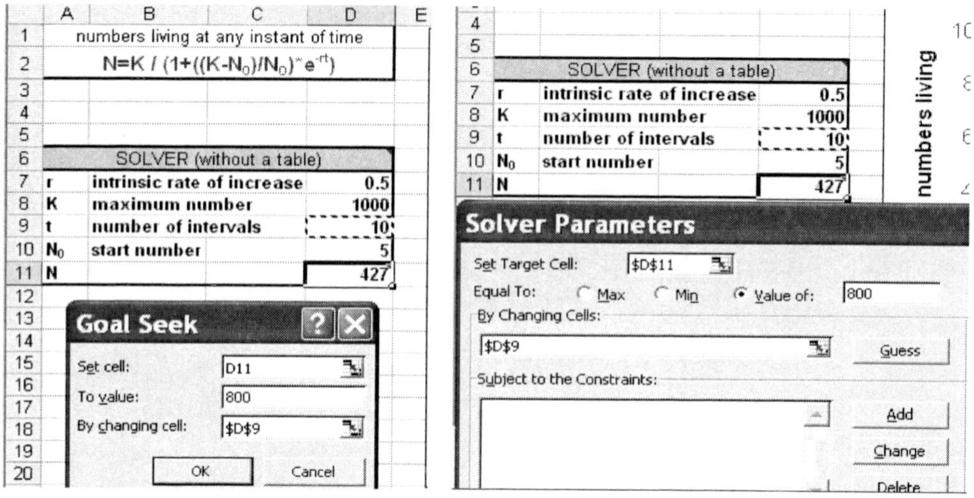

Can we find out in how many intervals (or generations), the maximum population size of 1000 will be reached (with r being 0.5)? Sure we can. Let us use only Solver this time:

1. Target Cell: D11 (this can only be one cell, N, and this cell must be a formula); D11 should be set to 1000 (which is K here; a Target cannot be set to a cell's reference)

2. Changing Cells: D9 (this could be more than 1 cell, but in this case it's only r)

3. We don't need any constraint, because r is already set to 0.5 in cell D7, and you cannot put constraints on values that don't feature in Changing cells.

The solution is 74 generations (t) – which is a long time, especially when you discover in the graph that the maximum seems to be reached much sooner. Why is that? Because Solver works with a precision of 0.00001. After you set this precision option back to 0.1, a solution will be reached after only 42 generations!

Sometimes, things may get a bit more complicated. Let us use another example (see Figure - 77 and refer to Estimating with a t-Distribution on page 25). Based on a sample size of 15, we predict with a 95% confidence that the population mean will be between 6.78 and 6.82 – which is the sample's mean ± limit. We could use Solver to find a smaller limit, say 0.01. These are the steps:

1. Because it is important that the Target cell holds a formula, start by locating your formulas: *Edit / GoTo / Special button / ⊙ Formulas*

2. The cells G5:L5 turn out to be based on formulas. Only one of these cells (yes, only one) is a potential Target for Solver.

3. Set J5 as a Target cell to 0.01 (you could also have set K5 to 6.79, or L5 to 6.81 – but Target only accepts one setting).

4. Which cells can be changed by Solver? The answer is, all cells used by the Target's formula! Usually, you want only a selection of these cells, though. In our case, we may be willing to change the sample size (D5) and/or the confidence error (G5). Let's do both.

5. However, we also want to keep the error below 3%. So add a constraint saying: G5<=3%. This constraint is possible because G5 is one of the changing cells.

6. Sometimes Solver cannot find a solution because your requests are impossible, or one of your settings is incompatible with another setting.

7. In this case, Solver provides a solution: 78.23. So we need a sample of at least 79 cases to reach a limit of 0.01 with only 3% chance of error.

Figure - 77

This example was also used in Figure - 24. Based on a sample size of 15, we predict with a 95% confidence that the population mean will be between 6.78 and 6.82 – which is the sample's mean ± limit. We can use Solver to find a smaller limit.

	A	B	C	D	E	F	G	H	I	J	K	L
1		SAMPLES						Confidence			Mean	
2	Feature	Mean	StDev	Count		Level	Error	t-Value	StErr	Limit	Min	Max
3												
4												
5	pH	6.8	0.04	15		95%	5%	2.1448	0.0103	0.0222	6.77785	6.8222
6												

One more example: Two sets of linear equations that need to be solved (see Figure - 78).

Where are the formulas? In cells A6 and A9 for the first pair, and in cells F6 and F9 for the second pair of linear equations.

Let's start with the first pair to the left:

> The Target cell A6 should be set to 5. There is only one Target cell possible, so the other formula (A9) must be handled with a constraint.

> The cells that are going to change are in C3 and D3.

> There is one constraint: A9=19

The solution is shown at the bottom of Figure - 78.

Do something similar for the second pair of linear equations.

Figure - 78

Two pairs of linear equations need a solution that can be found by *Solver*.

	A	B	C	D	E	F	G
1							
2			x	y			
3			?	?			
4							
5	3x+16y=5					2/3x+3/5y=17	
6	#VALUE!					#VALUE!	
7							
8	-5x+28y=19					3/4x+2/3y=19	
9	#VALUE!					#VALUE!	
10							
11	Solution:					Solution:	
12	x=-1 ; y=0.5					x=12 ; y=15	
13							

INTERMEZZO

If you ever need to "type" complicated equations, you can get help from a special tool in Excel.

You will find it under *Insert / Object*:

Microsoft Equation 3.0

or CorelEquation 11.

This tool allows you to "draw" and "type" professional looking equations. Just experiment with it.

Figure - 79

This is the way the Equation Editor looks and works.

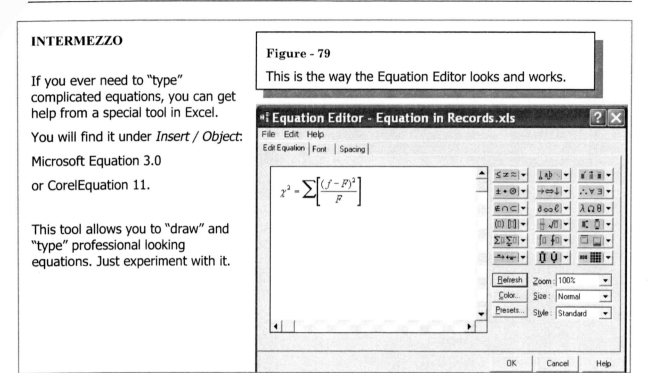

Table - 38 Options settings for Solver

Option	Purpose
Max time	Limits the time taken by the solution process. While you can enter a value as high as 32,767, the default value of 100 (seconds) is adequate for most small problems.
Iterations	Limits the time taken by the solution process by limiting the number of interim calculations. While you can enter a value as high as 32,767, the default value of 100 is adequate for most small problems.
Precision	Controls the precision of solutions by using the number you enter to determine whether the value of a constraint cell meets a target or satisfies a lower or upper bound. Precision must be indicated by a fractional number between 0 (zero) and 1. Higher precision is indicated when the number you enter has more decimal places — for example, 0.0001 is higher precision than 0.01.
Tolerance	The percentage by which the target cell of a solution satisfying the integer constraints can differ from the true optimal value and still be considered acceptable. This option applies only to problems with integer constraints. A higher tolerance tends to speed up the solution process.
Convergence	When the relative change in the target cell value is less than the number in the Convergence box for the last five iterations, Solver stops. Convergence applies only to nonlinear problems and must be indicated by a fractional number between 0 (zero) and 1. A smaller convergence is indicated when the number you enter has more decimal places — for example, 0.0001 is less relative change than 0.01. The smaller the convergence value, the more time Solver takes to reach a solution.

Option	Purpose
Assume Linear Model	Select to speed the solution process when all relationships in the model are linear and you want to solve a linear optimization problem.
Show Iteration Results	Select to have Solver pause to show the results of each iteration.
Use Automatic Scaling	Select to use automatic scaling when inputs and outputs have large differences in magnitude — for example, when maximizing the percentage of profit based on million-dollar investments.
Assume Non-Negative	Causes Solver to assume a lower limit of 0 (zero) for all adjustable cells for which you have not set a lower limit in the Constraint box in the Add Constraint dialog box.
Estimates	Specifies the approach used to obtain initial estimates of the basic variables in each one-dimensional search.
Tangent	Uses linear extrapolation from a tangent vector.
Quadratic	Uses quadratic extrapolation, which can improve the results on highly nonlinear problems.
Derivatives	Specifies the differencing used to estimate partial derivatives of the objective and constraint functions.
Forward	Use for most problems in which the constraint values change relatively slowly.
Central	Use for problems in which the constraints change rapidly, especially near the limits. Although this option requires more calculations, it might help when Solver returns a message that it could not improve the solution.
Search	Specifies the algorithm used at each iteration to determine the direction to search.
Newton	Uses a quasi-Newton method that typically requires more memory but fewer iterations than the Conjugate gradient method.
Conjugate	Requires less memory than the Newton method but typically needs more iterations to reach a particular level of accuracy. Use this option when you have a large problem and memory usage is a concern, or when stepping through iterations reveals slow progress.

Controls for Solving Equations

Instead of using GoalSeek or Solver, you can test your model by creating an extensive table and keeping all variables "under control." This time, we use a simpler formula called the logistic equation: $R = rN(1-N/K)$.

The table shown in Figure - 80 simulates the population growth for successive intervals or generations (t in column A) by adding R (in column D) to the existing number of individuals (N_t in column B).

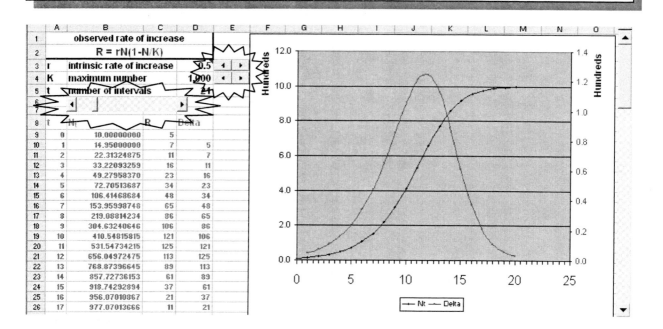

Figure - 80 The table to the left – and, consequently, the graph to the right – are both controlled by the controls that set variables.

Because the table in Figure - 80 is based on variables placed in the cells D3:D5, we can manipulate those variables and watch the results change in the table and/or graph. This manipulation can easily be achieved by using Controls in E3, E4, and B6:C7.

Figure - 81

Controls are created from the *Control Box* toolbar and are set from a *Properties* listing.

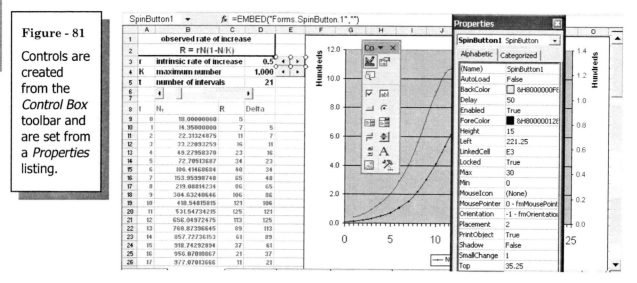

To implement *Controls*, you need to perform the following actions:

1. Add a new toolbar: *View / Toolbars / Control Toolbox*.
2. Click on the tool you want: Spin Button, Scroll Bar, or …
3. Draw this Control on your spreadsheet.
4. Click on the second button on the Toolbar to display Properties.

5. Set at least the following three properties for each Control:
    ➢ Min (its minimum value)
    ➢ Max (its maximum value)
    ➢ Linked Cell (the cell to display the Control's value; typing not clicking)
6. Close the Properties box.
7. Click on the first button on the Toolbar (green). This will close the design mode and put you back on the sheet.
8. Now you can test the Control.

Because Controls only use integers and therefore change by values of one, you must use a trick to handle decimals. For example, let's take the Control in cell E3 (see Figure - 81). If you want it to cover the range between 0.1 and 3.0, set the Control's Min to 1 and its Max to 30. Link the Control to a cell hidden behind the control (E3); and place the formula =E3/10 in cell D3 (the cell that you really want to manipulate).

If you make sure that the linked cells are hooked up to the table and that the table is hooked up to a graph, you will see dramatic changes in the graph once you manipulate your Controls. This is a visual and quick way of testing your models and equations for specific ranges of values.

Table - 39 A listing of Excel's Math and Trigonometry Functions

Function	Action
ABS	Returns the absolute value of a number
ACOS	Returns the arccosine of a number
ACOSH	Returns the inverse hyperbolic cosine of a number
ASIN	Returns the arcsine of a number
ASINH	Returns the inverse hyperbolic sine of a number
ATAN	Returns the arctangent of a number
ATAN2	Returns the arctangent from x- and y-coordinates
ATANH	Returns the inverse hyperbolic tangent of a number
CEILING	Rounds a number to the nearest integer or to the nearest multiple of significance
COMBIN	Returns the number of combinations for a given number of objects
COS	Returns the cosine of a number
COSH	Returns the hyperbolic cosine of a number
COUNTIF	Counts the number of nonblank cells within a range that meet the given criteria
DEGREES	Converts radians to degrees
EVEN	Rounds a number up to the nearest even integer
EXP	Returns e raised to the power of a given number

Function	Action
FACT	Returns the factorial of a number
FACTDOUBLE	Returns the double factorial of a number
FLOOR	Rounds a number down, toward zero
GCD	Returns the greatest common divisor
INT	Rounds a number down to the nearest integer
LCM	Returns the least common multiple
LN	Returns the natural logarithm of a number
LOG	Returns the logarithm of a number to a specified base
LOG10	Returns the base-10 logarithm of a number
MDETERM	Returns the matrix determinant of an array
MINVERSE	Returns the matrix inverse of an array
MMULT	Returns the matrix product of two arrays
MOD	Returns the remainder from division
MROUND	Returns a number rounded to the desired multiple
MULTINOMIAL	Returns the multinomial of a set of numbers
ODD	Rounds a number up to the nearest odd integer
PI	Returns the value of pi
POWER	Returns the result of a number raised to a power
PRODUCT	Multiplies its arguments
QUOTIENT	Returns the integer portion of a division
RADIANS	Converts degrees to radians
RAND	Returns a random number between 0 and 1
RANDBETWEEN	Returns a random number between the numbers you specify
ROMAN	Converts an arabic numeral to roman, as text
ROUND	Rounds a number to a specified number of digits
ROUNDDOWN	Rounds a number down, toward zero
ROUNDUP	Rounds a number up, away from zero
SERIESSUM	Returns the sum of a power series based on the formula
SIGN	Returns the sign of a number
SIN	Returns the sine of the given angle
SINH	Returns the hyperbolic sine of a number
SQRT	Returns a positive square root
SQRTPI	Returns the square root of (number * pi)

V

Function	Action
SUBTOTAL	Returns a subtotal in a list or database
SUM	Adds its arguments
SUMIF	Adds the cells specified by a given criteria
SUMPRODUCT	Returns the sum of the products of corresponding array components
SUMSQ	Returns the sum of the squares of the arguments
SUMX2MY2	Returns the sum of the difference of squares of corresponding values in two arrays
SUMX2PY2	Returns the sum of the sum of squares of corresponding values in two arrays
SUMXMY2	Returns the sum of squares of differences of corresponding values in two arrays
TAN	Returns the tangent of a number
TANH	Returns the hyperbolic tangent of a number
TRUNC	Truncates a number to an integer

 Exercise 39.

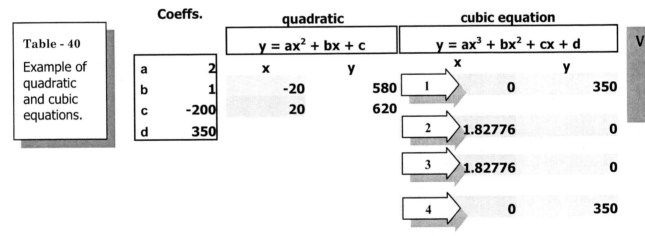

Table - 40	Coeffs.		quadratic $y = ax^2 + bx + c$		cubic equation $y = ax^3 + bx^2 + cx + d$	
			x	y	x	y
Example of quadratic and cubic equations.	a	2	-20	580	1 → 0	350
	b	1	20	620		
	c	-200			2 → 1.82776	0
	d	350			3 → 1.82776	0
					4 → 0	350

1. Using formulas in the columns for Y, type the data from Table - 40.

2. Apply Goalseek to the quadratic equation in order to find its roots – that is, where the curve crosses the X-axis at Y=0). Use Solver to find its minimum.

3. Use Solver for the cubic equation:

   a. For line 1: set y=0 by changing x

   b. For line 2: the same but with constraint x < -5

   c. For line 3: the same but with constraint x > 5

   d. For line 4: set y=0 (and x=0) by changing the coefficients a, b, c, and d.

4. Create an XY-chart for the quadratic equation $y = ax^2 + bx + c$ between X=−20 and X=20 (with intervals of 5; see Figure - 82).

Figure - 82

XY graph for a quadratic equation.

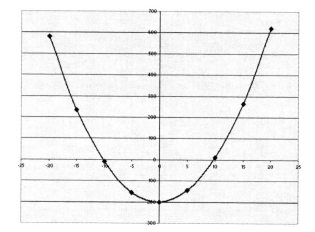

5. Create an XY-chart for the cubic equation $y = ax^3 + bx^2 + cx + d$ between X=−20 and X=20 (with intervals of 5; see Figure - 83).

Figure - 83

XY graph for a cubic equation

V

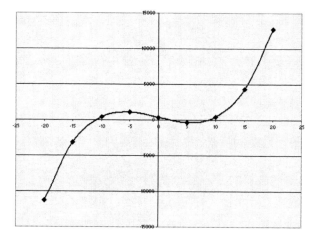

Chapter VI: Data Analysis

Validation

To make sure that the data entered into your research records are valid, you need some kind of validation. Without validation, users can enter whatever they want into a cell. After validation, there is some form of data entry checking on your spreadsheets.

Here is one way to do validation:

1. Type a list of valid entries on a separate sheet.
2. Assign a Name to the list (see Naming Cells on page 6).
3. Go to the cell(s) in need of validation.
4. Select Validation in the Data menu.
5. For Allow, select List.
6. For Source, select =myList (the equal sign creates a reference to the range so named!)

Figure - 84

The dialog box for Data Validation can be set, among other things, to a List (and its Source), or to Custom (and its formula).

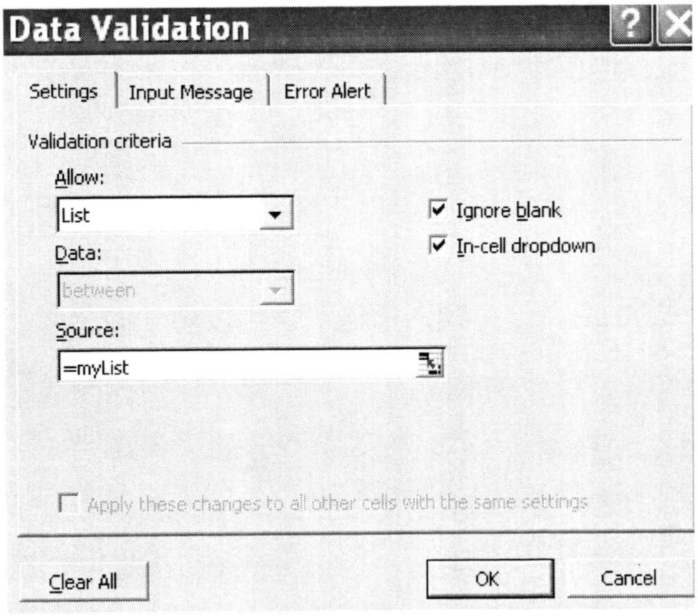

Tip:

The Allow option also accepts Custom settings.

Let's say that you want only those values in cell A1 that range between 1 and 100. The formula would be:

=AND(A1>0, A1<=100).

Or perhaps, you want cell A1 to only accept values between the minimum and maximum of values in column B:

=AND(A1>=MIN(B:B),A1<=MAX(B:B)).

Sorting Records

Rule #1: A table of records is demarcated by an entirely empty row and an entirely empty column (empty cells are OK). So avoid empty rows and columns inside your table, for those would create TWO or more tables, which would sort independently.

Rule #2: In order to sort by a specific column, do NOT select the total column, for you would only sort what is in that column, and the rest of the records would remain in place. Instead, select ONE cell in that column (or its label) and hit the A-Z or Z-A button.

Rule #3: If you want to sort by more than one column, go to *Data / Sort* to sort by up to three criteria.

Rule #4: If you need more than three criteria, apply rule #3 for the last three criteria, and then apply Sort again for the first one(s).

Rule #5: If you want to sort by a specific order that is not alphabetically oriented, use Data / Sort again, but this time hit the Options button, which allows you to use a specific order list – which you may have created under *Tools / Option / CustomLists* (see Filling Adjacent Cells on page 3).

Figure - 85

The Data/Sort menu allows up to three sorting criteria, including a sort option based on a (customized) list.

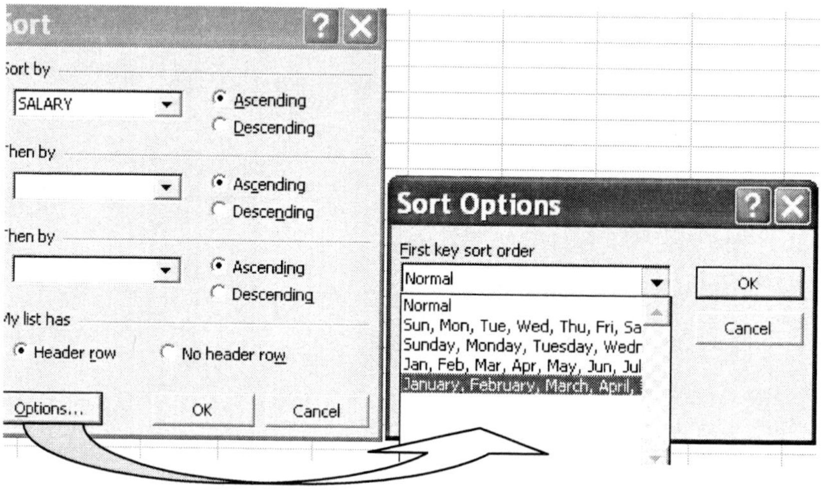

Creating Subtotals

There are times when you want to create subtotals in your research records. Let's take the database from Figure - 86 as an example.

Figure - 86

An example of a database that may need subtotals

	A	B	C	D	E	F	G	H	I
1	Plate ID	Analyst	50 ng/mL	%CV	25 ng/mL	%CV	10 ng/mL	%CV	
2	8877p58a	gmv	47.7	2	22.7	0	10.3	0	
3			48.7	3	23.0	3	10.0	0	
4			49.3	0	23.0	1	10.4	3	
5			45.9	2.0	22.9	1.0	9.8	1.0	
6	8877p58b	tkm	47.5	0	22.7	2	9.6	8	
7			45.9	1	22.9	3	9.4	0	
8			43.2	4	22.6	3	9.6	4	
9			44.3	3.0	20.7	3.0	9.7	6.0	
10	8696p08a	ksm	56.4	12	29.1	11	12.8	9	
11			51.3	2	26.9	1	11.7	1	
12			52.3	1	26.5	2	12.2	2	
13			49.7	2.0	25.0	1.0	11.2	3.0	
14	8696p08b	bdo	52.9	3	27.5	6	13.1	9	
15			50.1	1	26.8	3	12.1	2	
16			51.0	1	26.1	1	12.3	2	
17			48.6	1.0	24.8	0.0	11.4	2.0	
18	8697p58b	tjk	47.5	0	22.7	2	9.6	8	
19			47.5	1	22.9	3	9.4	0	
20			43.2	4	22.6	3	9.4	4	
21			44.3	3.0	22.6	3.0	9.4	6.0	
22									

If there are empty cells below each category, you need to fill them first:

1. Select columns A and B.

2. Select *Edit / GoTo / Special button / ⊙ Blanks / OK.*

3. Do not click anywhere, but immediately start typing the formula =A1 (which means: the cell above me) in the first cell of the selection.

4. Place the =A1 formula in all selected cells: Ctrl + Enter.

5. Select columns A and B again.

6. Replace all formulas with their values: *Copy / Paste Special / ⊙ Values / Esc.*

Now that all cells are filled, we can insert subtotals at the end of each PlateID:

1. Click inside the database.

2. Select *Data / Subtotals.*

3. Select *At each change in: PlateID*

4. Select *Use function: Sum or StDev*

5. Select *Add subtotal to:* Select the columns you want to summarize (e.g. ng/ml 3x).

6. Click OK.

Figure - 87 The database shown in Figure - 86 has been outfitted with an outline (to the left) that allows switching between summaries and details.

		A	B	C	D	E	F	G	H	I	J
	1	Plate ID	Analyst	50 ng/mL	%CV	25 ng/mL	%CV	10 ng/mL	%CV		
+	6	8877p58a Average		47.9		22.9		10.1			
+	11	8877p58b Average		45.2		22.2		9.6			
+	16	8696p08a Average		52.4		26.9		12.0			
+	21	8696p08b Average		50.7		26.3		12.2			
·	22	8697p58b	tjk	47.5	0	22.7	2	9.6	8		
·	23	8697p58b	tjk	47.5	1	22.9	3	9.4	0		
·	24	8697p58b	tjk	43.2	4	22.6	3	9.4	4		
·	25	8697p58b	tjk	44.3	3.0	22.6	3.0	9.4	6.0		
−	26	8697p58b Average		45.6		22.7		9.5			
−	27	Grand Average		48.4		24.2		10.7			
	28										
	29										
	30										

Notice the outline in front of the first column in Figure - 87:

➢ Clicking on button 2 allows you to collapse all the details.

➢ Clicking on button 1 shows only the overall figures.

➢ Clicking on any + button opens up the details for that section

➢ Clicking on any − button closes the details of that section

If you want to add another kind of subtotal:

1. Once again, select *Data / Subtotals.*

2. Change the function, or whatever you want to alter.

3. Don't forget to uncheck ❑ Replace current subtotal (not ☑).

If you had different analysts working on the same plates, you could go down one more level:

➢ To split PlateID per Analyst: Sort by PlateID first, then by Analyst (see Figure 88)

➢ To split Analyst per PlateID: Sort by Analyst first, then by PlateID

VI

Figure - 88

The outline has been expanded with one more level: a split per Analyst inside a split per PlateID.

			A	B	C	D	E	F	G	H
		1	Plate ID	Analyst	50 ng/mL	%CV	25 ng/mL	%CV	10 ng/mL	%CV
		4		gmv Average	48.2		22.9		10.2	
		7		tjk Average	47.6		23.0		10.1	
		8	8877p58a Average		47.9		22.9		10.1	
		11		tkm Average	46.7		22.8		9.5	
		14		gmv Average	43.8		21.7		9.7	
		15	8877p58b Average		45.2		22.2		9.6	
		18		bdo Average	53.9		28.0		12.3	
		21		ksm Average	51.0		25.8		11.7	
		22	8696p08a Average		52.4		26.9		12.0	
		25		tjk Average	51.5		27.2		12.6	
		28		bdo Average	49.8		25.5		11.9	
		29	8696p08b Average		50.7		26.3		12.2	
		32		tjk Average	47.5		22.8		9.5	
		35		gmv Average	43.8		22.6		9.4	
		36	8697p58b Average		45.6		22.7		9.5	
		37		Grand Average	48.4		24.2		10.7	
		38	Grand Average		48.4		24.2		10.7	
		39								
		40								

It almost speaks for itself that any graph hooked up to this table reflects either the total or the summary information, according to the choices made in your table.

Figure - 89 Graphs hooked up to a table with outlines reflect the settings of the outlines.

Table with no subtotals per plate

Table with subtotals per plate included

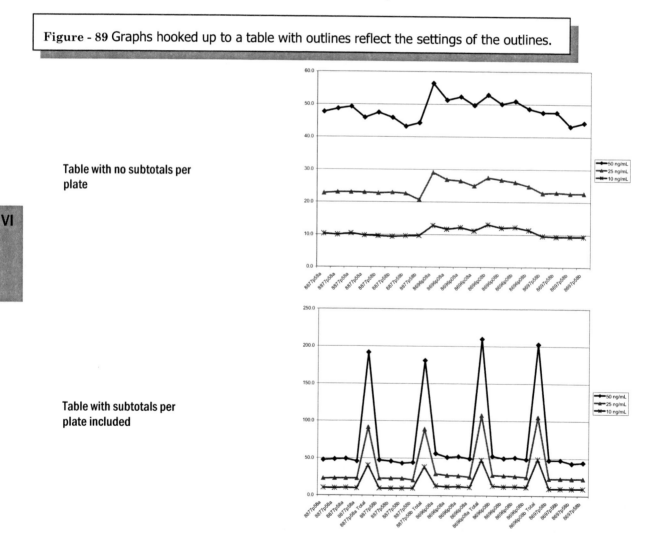

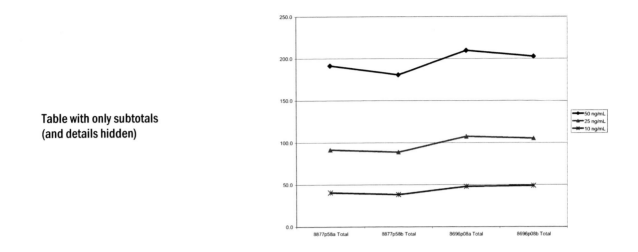

Table with only subtotals (and details hidden)

Using Data Filters

When you have thousands of records with measurements, you may want to analyze specific subsets of those records. That's where *filters* come in (Figure - 90):

The most flexible filters should be created outside of your table of records – that is, at least two rows below it or on a separate sheet.

Figure - 90

The labels of the database (on top) are used as labels for the filter (at the bottom).

	A	B	C	D	E	F
1	Patient	DOB	Age	Height	Systolic	
2	Bush	1/1/1969	35	1.73	1	
3	Carter	8/8/1938	65	1.79	139	
4	Clinton	5/5/1922	82	1.85	160	
5	Eisenhower	3/3/1950	54	1.63	148	
6	Ford	2/2/1948	56	1.72	155	
7	Johnson	1/1/1958	46	1.89	145	
8	Kennedy	9/9/1939	64	1.78	137	
9	Nixon	7/7/1947	57	1.75	155	
10	Reagan	4/4/1954	50	1.82	137	
11						
12						
13	Patient	DOB	Age	Height	Systolic	
14			<60		>140	
15						

To start filtering:

1. Repeat the table's labels for your filter.

2. Add some criteria directly below the filter's labels.

3. Click inside the main table.

4. Select *Data / Filter / Advanced Filter*.

5. Select the proper ranges + click OK.

To stop filtering:

1. Select *Data / Filter / Show All*.

VI

There are some important rules and information you need to know for your filters (Figure - 91):

🧪 AND conditions should be on the same row (e.g. Age<60 AND SBP>140)

🧪 OR conditions should be on the next row (e.g. first row under SBP: >140, second row: <100)

🧪 If you want Age<60 AND at the same time Age>50, add another Age column

🧪 All rows and columns in a filter should be contiguous, so completely empty rows or columns are never allowed inside the filter; they create errors

🧪 The problem with filtered subsets is that they need to be updated each time there is a change in criteria

Figure - 91

In criteria filters, AND conditions should be on the same row, whereas OR conditions are on separate rows.

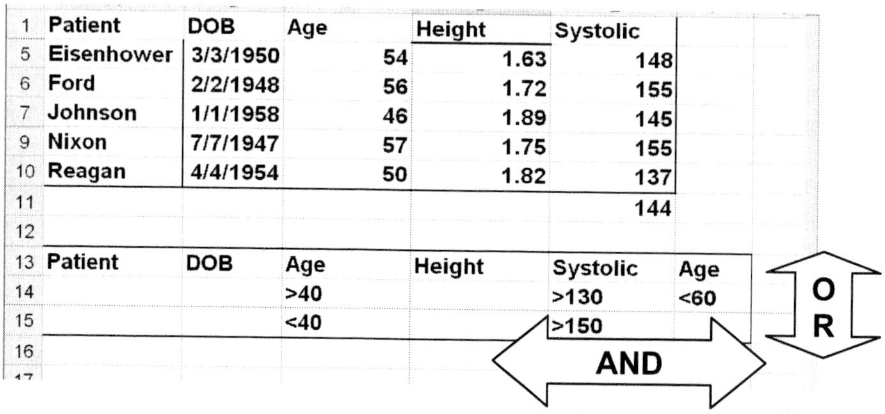

1	Patient	DOB	Age	Height	Systolic	
5	Eisenhower	3/3/1950	54	1.63	148	
6	Ford	2/2/1948	56	1.72	155	
7	Johnson	1/1/1958	46	1.89	145	
9	Nixon	7/7/1947	57	1.75	155	
10	Reagan	4/4/1954	50	1.82	137	
11					144	
12						
13	Patient	DOB	Age	Height	Systolic	Age
14			>40		>130	<60
15			<40		>150	
16						
17						

AND **OR**

Database Functions

There are times that you do not want to visually "carve out" the records that meet certain criteria. All you may need is basic summary information regarding a certain subset of records.

The common functions such as SUM(), AVERAGE(), COUNT(), and STDEV() do not help you here because they work on <u>all</u> records. However, there are D-functions, such as **DSUM**, **DAVERAGE**, and **DSTDEV**, that allow you to specify certain criteria and perform calculations on those specific records.

All database functions have the same syntax:

=DFUNCTION(database, field, criteria)

➤ *Database*: the (name of the) range where the records are located (including their labels)

➤ *Field*: perform the calculation on a specific field - either by column # in the database (with or without the MATCH function) or the address/name of its label

➤ *Criteria*: the (name of the) range where the criteria are located (including labels)

In Figure - 92, we used several database functions: DCOUNT(), DMIN(), DMAX(), DAVERAGE().().().All of them use the same database range and criteria range, but they perform their calculations on a different field.

Figure - 92

Databases and filter criteria can be used together in so-called *Database Functions* (DSUM, etc.)

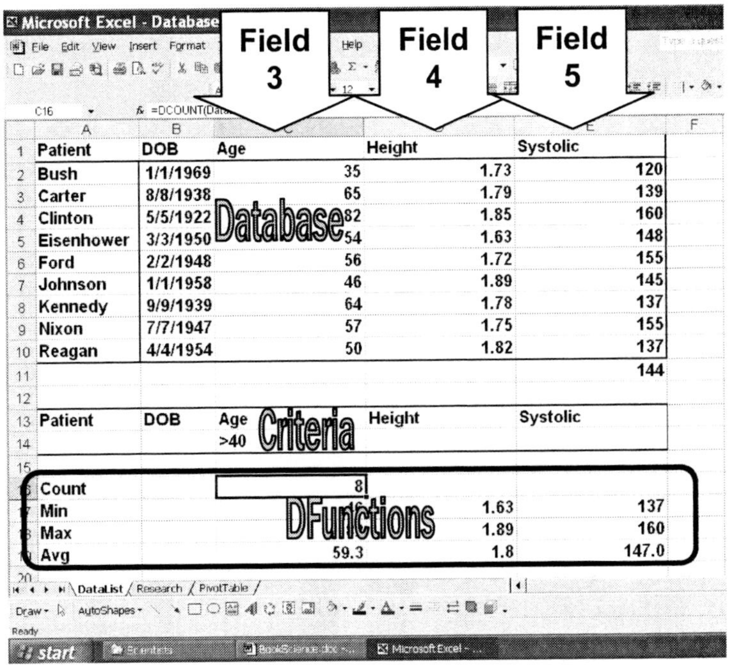

One nice thing about database functions is the fact that their results update immediately when records or criteria change.

However, they do not update when you add new rows at the bottom of your database or filter range, unless you use dynamic range names (see Working with Dynamic Ranges on page 57).

Figure - 93

It is possible to give your database a dynamic range name, which adjusts automatically when rows and columns at the end are added or deleted.

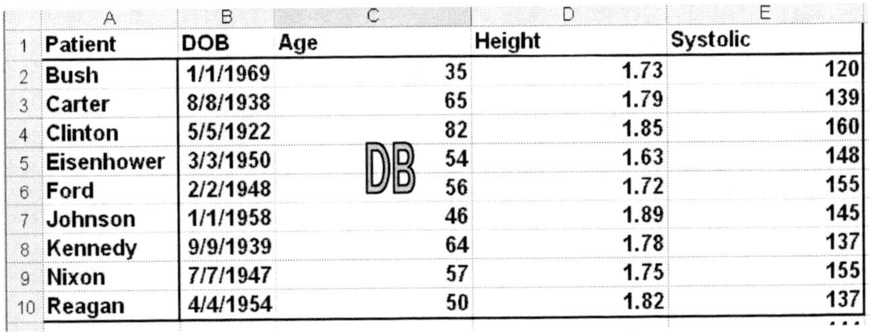

VI

This is the way to create a <u>dynamic</u> range under the name DB (see Figure - 93):

1. *Insert / Name / Define*: DB

2. Reference: =**offset**(Sheet1!$A$1,0,0,**counta**(Sheet1!$A:$A),**counta**(Sheet1!$1:$1))

From now on, you must make sure you do not have any other cells with content somewhere in the first row or first column of this sheet. Consequently, you must place your filters on another sheet, or at least outside the first row and first column. That may be a high price to pay.

In case you are interested, there is one more solution. Name the range "Database" (and only that name!) and use the menu *Data / Form* to enter new records. This form adds new records at the end and then automatically resizes the range named Database. However, this solution will not help you if you add a new column at the end.

Calculated Criteria

The criteria we have used so far are all based on simple <u>comparison</u> operators such as >, >=, <, and <=.

In addition to comparison filters, you may need also <u>computed</u> filters. Computed filters are based on calculations, so they start with an equal sign followed by functions and regular comparison operators.

Say you want to filter for records of people who are more than 50 years old – which is a <u>comparison</u> filter – and who are also below the average systolic blood pressure – which is a <u>computed</u> filter. In order to do so, we need a new column in our criteria range:

1. Add a label with a new name.
2. Refer to the first value in a database column as relative.
3. Refer to a specific range in the database as absolute ($-signs using F4).

In this case, we could add a new label, BPLow, to the criteria range (see Figure - 94). The formula under it reads:

= E2 < AVERAGE($E$2:$E$10)

The formula evaluates to true or false depending on whether this is actually true or false for the corresponding cell of the first record in the database (E2). But the formula will work for all other records in the database as well.

Figure - 94

Criteria filters also accept computed criteria. All they need is a label and a proper formula.

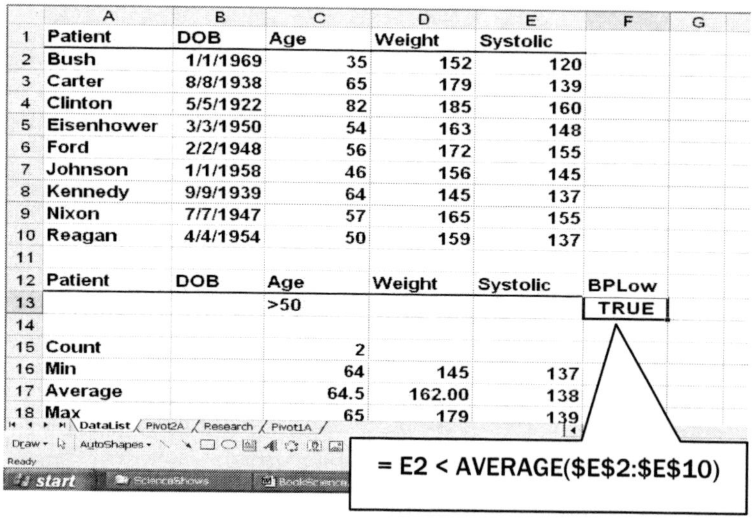

	A	B	C	D	E	F	G
1	Patient	DOB	Age	Weight	Systolic		
2	Bush	1/1/1969	35	152	120		
3	Carter	8/8/1938	65	179	139		
4	Clinton	5/5/1922	82	185	160		
5	Eisenhower	3/3/1950	54	163	148		
6	Ford	2/2/1948	56	172	155		
7	Johnson	1/1/1958	46	156	145		
8	Kennedy	9/9/1939	64	145	137		
9	Nixon	7/7/1947	57	165	155		
10	Reagan	4/4/1954	50	159	137		
11							
12	Patient	DOB	Age	Weight	Systolic	BPLow	
13			>50			TRUE	
14							
15	Count		2				
16	Min		64	145	137		
17	Average		64.5	162.00	138		
18	Max		65	179	139		

All database <u>functions</u> automatically update – provided that their filter range does include the new filter column. If you want to actually see the subset of records that happen to meet these conditions, use *Data / Filter / Advanced Filter.*

Here are a few more examples of computed filter settings such as you see used in Figure - 95:

=D2>AVERAGE($D$2:$D$22)	Filters only for C-Values above average
=COUNTIF($C$2:$C$22,C2)>2	Filters only for analysts who have more than two records
=COUNTIF($D$2:$D$22,D2)>1	Filters only for records that show duplicate C-Values

	A	B	C	D	E	F
1	Plate ID	Date	Analyst	C Value	Max OD	
2	8696p08d	09/14/01	cod	59.9	2.3	
3	8877p63a	09/14/01	cod	45.0	2.8	
4	8877p120e	10/03/01	ejs	62.5	1.5	
5	8877p66b	09/26/01	ejs	47.5	2.6	
6	8877p78b	09/21/01	ejs	60.8	2.8	
7	8696p08b	09/14/01	etv	62.5	2.4	
8	8877p60a	09/12/01	etv	58.3	3.2	
9	8877p71b	09/19/01	etv	79.4	2.5	
10	8877p84b	09/25/01	etv	78.4	1.9	
11	8877p70c	09/18/01	gmv	57.1	1.4	
12	8877p83a	09/25/01	gmv	83.7	2.0	
13	8696p08e	09/14/01	kpm	73.6	2.5	
14	8877p58a	09/11/01	kpm	64.8	2.6	
15	8877p63b	09/14/01	kpm	50.2	2.7	
16	8877p75b	09/20/01	kpm	58.4	1.7	
17	8696p08f	09/14/01	luv	63.3	2.4	
18	8877p66a	09/26/01	luv	45.4	2.8	
19	8877p78a	09/21/01	luv	65.8	2.6	
20						
21	Plate ID	Date	Analyst	C Value	Max OD	OverAvgC
22						FALSE
23						
24	Plate ID	Date	Analyst	C Value	Max OD	Anal>2Recs
25						FALSE
26						
27	Plate ID	Date	Analyst	C Value	Max OD	Dupl. CVal.
28						FALSE
29						

Figure - 95

This list of records was used for three different computed filters.

Marked Records

In order to locate specific records in a database, it may come in handy to mark certain records whenever some value exceeds certain criteria. This can be done with *conditional formatting*:

1. Select the cells (or column) of values that you want to watch.
2. Select *Format / Conditional Formatting* (see Figure - 96).
3. Select a comparison option.
4. Fill in a value.
5. Click the Format button.
6. Choose your new format.

Now all cells that qualify will show the new format – even when they change!

Figure - 96

This is the Conditional Formating dialog box.

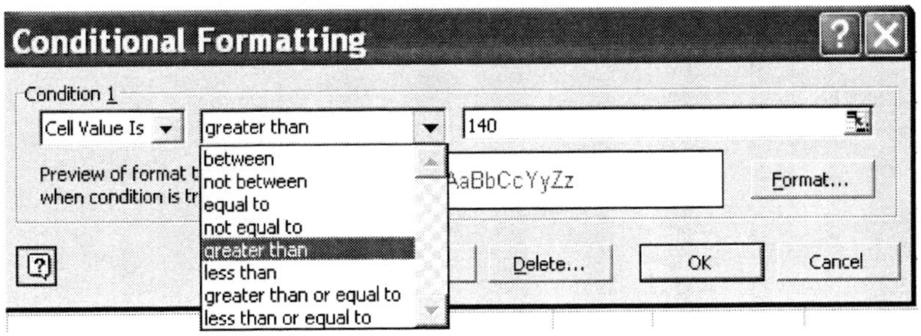

The box for conditional formatting also accepts <u>formulas</u>. Say you want to mark each second record with a gray background color for readability purposes. These are the steps:

1. Select the entire database.
2. Go to: *Format / Conditional Formatting*
3. In first box, select *Formula Is.*
4. In the second box, find out the row number of each record with the ROW() function.
5. Apply the MOD() function to find the remainder of the row number divided by 2:
   MOD(4, 2) returns 0,
   whereas MOD(5, 2) returns 1
6. If this remainder equals 0, then we have an even row number: 2, 4, etc. So the formula is:

   = MOD(ROW() , 2) = 0

7. Now set the format: On the *Patterns* tab, select a background color (Figure - 97).

Figure - 97

Conditional Formatting based on a formula that uses the MOD function

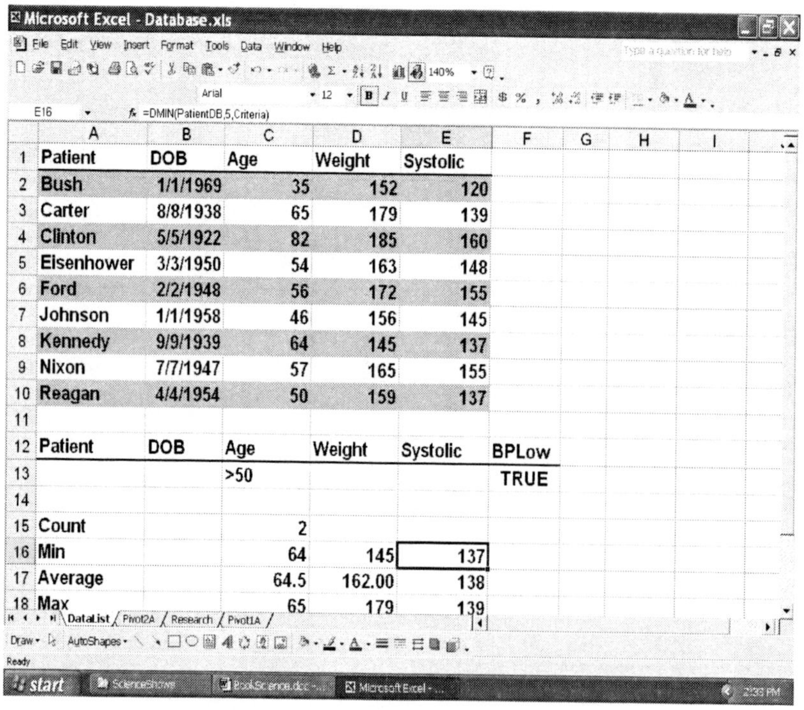

	A	B	C	D	E	F
1	Patient	DOB	Age	Weight	Systolic	
2	Bush	1/1/1969	35	152	120	
3	Carter	8/8/1938	65	179	139	
4	Clinton	5/5/1922	82	185	160	
5	Eisenhower	3/3/1950	54	163	148	
6	Ford	2/2/1948	56	172	155	
7	Johnson	1/1/1958	46	156	145	
8	Kennedy	9/9/1939	64	145	137	
9	Nixon	7/7/1947	57	165	155	
10	Reagan	4/4/1954	50	159	137	
11						
12	Patient	DOB	Age	Weight	Systolic	BPLow
13			>50			TRUE
14						
15	Count		2			
16	Min		64	145	137	
17	Average		64.5	162.00	138	
18	Max		65	179	139	

The *Formula-Is* option in the Conditional Formatting dialog box also allows for more sophisticated settings. Here are some examples:

=C2<>C1	This is the formula for range *C2:C22* in Figure - 98. It would mark each first record for a new analyst.
=COUNTIF($D$2:$D$22,D2)>1	This is the formula for range *D2:D22* in Figure - 98. It would mark duplicate records with a specific format.

Here are some additional rules:

○ If you use conditional formatting for a <u>sub</u>-range and then another setting for the <u>total</u> range, the latter one takes over.

○ The conditional formats for separate sub-ranges don't "bite" each other.

○ If you use the Add option, you can specify up to three conditions for the same range, but the <u>first</u> condition reigns. So make this one the "strongest" condition – for instance: first D2>60, then D2>50.

<table>
<tr><td></td><td>A</td><td>B</td><td>C</td><td>D</td><td>E</td></tr>
<tr><td>1</td><td>Plate ID</td><td>Date</td><td>Analyst</td><td>C Value</td><td>Max OD</td></tr>
<tr><td>2</td><td>8696p08d</td><td>09/14/01</td><td>cod</td><td>59.9</td><td>2.3</td></tr>
<tr><td>3</td><td>8877p63a</td><td>09/14/01</td><td>cod</td><td>45.0</td><td>2.8</td></tr>
<tr><td>4</td><td>8877p120e</td><td>10/03/01</td><td>ejs</td><td>62.5</td><td>1.5</td></tr>
<tr><td>5</td><td>8877p66b</td><td>09/26/01</td><td>ejs</td><td>47.5</td><td>2.6</td></tr>
<tr><td>6</td><td>8877p78b</td><td>09/21/01</td><td>ejs</td><td>60.8</td><td>2.8</td></tr>
<tr><td>7</td><td>8696p08b</td><td>09/14/01</td><td>etv</td><td>62.5</td><td>2.4</td></tr>
<tr><td>8</td><td>8877p60a</td><td>09/12/01</td><td>etv</td><td>58.3</td><td>3.2</td></tr>
<tr><td>9</td><td>8877p71b</td><td>09/19/01</td><td>etv</td><td>79.4</td><td>2.5</td></tr>
<tr><td>10</td><td>8877p84b</td><td>09/25/01</td><td>etv</td><td>78.4</td><td>1.9</td></tr>
<tr><td>11</td><td>8877p70c</td><td>09/18/01</td><td>gmv</td><td>57.1</td><td>1.4</td></tr>
<tr><td>12</td><td>8877p83a</td><td>09/25/01</td><td>gmv</td><td>83.7</td><td>2.0</td></tr>
<tr><td>13</td><td>8696p08e</td><td>09/14/01</td><td>kpm</td><td>73.6</td><td>2.5</td></tr>
<tr><td>14</td><td>8877p58a</td><td>09/11/01</td><td>kpm</td><td>64.8</td><td>2.6</td></tr>
<tr><td>15</td><td>8877p63b</td><td>09/14/01</td><td>kpm</td><td>50.2</td><td>2.7</td></tr>
<tr><td>16</td><td>8877p75b</td><td>09/20/01</td><td>kpm</td><td>58.4</td><td>1.7</td></tr>
<tr><td>17</td><td>8696p08f</td><td>09/14/01</td><td>luv</td><td>63.3</td><td>2.4</td></tr>
<tr><td>18</td><td>8877p66a</td><td>09/26/01</td><td>luv</td><td>45.4</td><td>2.8</td></tr>
<tr><td>19</td><td>8877p78a</td><td>09/21/01</td><td>luv</td><td>65.8</td><td>2.6</td></tr>
<tr><td>20</td><td>8877p58b</td><td>09/11/01</td><td>tjk</td><td>70.2</td><td>2.2</td></tr>
<tr><td>21</td><td>8877p70d</td><td>09/18/01</td><td>tjk</td><td>39.8</td><td>1.1</td></tr>
<tr><td>22</td><td>8877p83b</td><td>09/25/01</td><td>tjk</td><td>64.9</td><td>1.7</td></tr>
<tr><td>23</td><td></td><td></td><td></td><td></td><td></td></tr>
</table>

Figure - 98

This listing of records was used to conditionally format duplicate values.

Exercise 40.

1. Create the table from Figure - 99.

Figure - 99

Filters can help you test several hypotheses on these records.

<table>
<tr><td></td><td>A</td><td>B</td><td>C</td><td>D</td><td>E</td><td>F</td><td>G</td></tr>
<tr><td>1</td><td>Group of lizards</td><td>sample size</td><td>°C Temp</td><td>Sex</td><td>rads Co⁶⁰ γ rays</td><td>life span in days</td><td>SD of span</td></tr>
<tr><td>2</td><td>1</td><td>50</td><td>18</td><td>M</td><td>0</td><td>55</td><td>1</td></tr>
<tr><td>3</td><td>2</td><td>50</td><td>18</td><td>F</td><td>0</td><td>65</td><td>2</td></tr>
<tr><td>4</td><td>3</td><td>50</td><td>18</td><td>M</td><td>10000</td><td>40</td><td>1</td></tr>
<tr><td>5</td><td>4</td><td>50</td><td>18</td><td>F</td><td>10000</td><td>65</td><td>2</td></tr>
<tr><td>6</td><td>5</td><td>50</td><td>20</td><td>M</td><td>10000</td><td>55</td><td>1</td></tr>
<tr><td>7</td><td>6</td><td>50</td><td>20</td><td>F</td><td>10000</td><td>75</td><td>2</td></tr>
<tr><td>8</td><td>7</td><td>50</td><td>20</td><td>M</td><td>0</td><td>65</td><td>2</td></tr>
<tr><td>9</td><td>8</td><td>50</td><td>20</td><td>F</td><td>0</td><td>75</td><td>2</td></tr>
</table>

2. To find the relationship between sex and life span, sort by Sex and Span.

3. To estimate the effect of radiation on life span sort by Sex and rads.

4. Get the original order back (without using the Undo button).

5. Add an advanced filter below the table (don't forget Rule #1).

6. Filter for females.

7. Calculate the mean, min, and max of the life span for females only.

8. Find out whether the mean, min, and max change for females when rads change from 0 to 10000.

9. Find out whether the mean changes for either sex with variations in temperature.

10. Highlight every female row with a gray pattern.

VI

Appendix A: Answers to Exercises

Exercise 2.

2. in C4: =B4-A4

3. format: h:mm:ss (if >24 hrs: [h]:mm:ss)

4. in E4: =D4/(C4*24)

Exercise 3.

2. 24.5; 2.55

4. 1; 2; 4; 2; 1

5. -1.4; -0.6; 0.2; 1; 1.8

6. 0.09; 0.28; 0.58; 0.84; 0.96

Exercise 4.

Z-value	Surface
-3.0	0%
-2.5	1%
-2.0	2%
-1.5	7%
-1.0	16%
-0.5	31%
0.0	50%
0.5	69%
1.0	84%
1.5	93%
2.0	98%
2.5	99%
3.0	100%

Exercise 6.

1. 1. 24

2. 2. 2.06

3. 3. 5%

4. 4. 2.5%

Exercise 7.

3. tdist

4. tdist($A2,B$1,1)

t-value one-tailed		2	4	6	8	10
	0	50.00%	50.00%	50.00%	50.00%	50.00%
	1	21.13%	18.70%	17.80%	17.33%	17.04%
	2	9.18%	5.81%	4.62%	4.03%	3.67%
	3	4.77%	2.00%	1.20%	0.85%	0.67%
	4	2.86%	0.81%	0.36%	0.20%	0.13%
	5	1.89%	0.37%	0.12%	0.05%	0.03%
	6	1.33%	0.19%	0.05%	0.02%	0.01%
	7	0.99%	0.11%	0.02%	0.01%	0.00%
	8	0.76%	0.07%	0.01%	0.00%	0.00%
	9	0.61%	0.04%	0.01%	0.00%	0.00%
	10	0.49%	0.03%	0.00%	0.00%	0.00%

Exercise 8.

1. 12%
2. 3

Exercise 9.

2. 1
3. 5.76%
4. 3.61
5. 3.84
6. 5.76%

Exercise 10.

chi-value		2	4	6	8	10
	0	100.00%	100.00%	100.00%	100.00%	100.00%
	1	60.65%	90.98%	98.56%	99.82%	99.98%
	2	36.79%	73.58%	91.97%	98.10%	99.63%
	...					
	17	0.02%	0.19%	0.93%	3.01%	7.44%
	18	0.01%	0.12%	0.62%	2.12%	5.50%
	19	0.01%	0.08%	0.42%	1.49%	4.03%
	20	0.00%	0.05%	0.28%	1.03%	2.93%

Exercise 11.

1. 1.96
2. 0.23
3. 0.45
4. 18.56 and 19.46

5. 95% confident

6. 5% risk

Exercise 12.

1. 2.06

2. 0.23

3. 0.48

4. 18.53 and 19.49

5. 95% confident

6. 5% risk

Exercise 13.

1. 12%

2. 0.03

3. 1.96

4. 0.06

5. 6% and 18%

Exercise 14.

1. 0.012

2. t-value

3. 1.67

4. 2.06

5. Yes

Exercise 15.

1. 20%

2. 50%

3. 5% level

4. 19

5. Yes

Exercise 16.

1. Each day: 103

2. 4

3. 0.075

4. 9.49

A

5. 8.49

6. No, 8.49<9.49

Exercise 17.

1. 5.76

2. 4.63

3. No, sample 1 is significantly more variable

Exercise 18.

1. Anova: Single Factor

2. Yes (9.45 > 4.10)

3. Highly unlikely: 0.5%

Exercise 19.

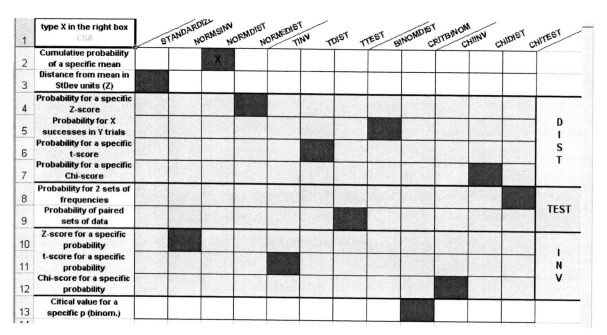

	type X in the right box CSA	STANDARDIZE	NORMSINV	NORMDIST	NORMSDIST	TINV	TDIST	TTEST	BINOMDIST	CRITBINOM	CHIINV	CHIDIST	CHITEST	
2	Cumulative probability of a specific mean			X										
3	Distance from mean in StDev units (Z)	■												
4	Probability for a specific Z-score				■									D
5	Probability for X successes in Y trials							■						I
6	Probability for a specific t-score						■							S
7	Probability for a specific Chi-score											■		T
8	Probability for 2 sets of frequencies												■	
9	Probability of paired sets of data							■						TEST
10	Z-score for a specific probability		■											
11	t-score for a specific probability					■								I N V
12	Chi-score for a specific probability										■			
13	Critical value for a specific p (binom.)									■				

Exercise 20.

1. t

2. p

3. Chi

4. Z

5. p

6. t

7. Chi

8. t

Exercise 21.

1. XY or Scatter

Exercise 25.

3. XY

Exercise 28.

3. y = 9.6904x (slope) + 30.345 (intercept)
   R2 = 0.8745 (R-squared value)

6. 0

Exercise 30.

The power of 5 gives good results, but the number of data is rather small here.

Exercise 32.

1. Use PEARSON (not CORREL):
   −0.98   0.25   0.92   1.00

2. Although weight has a low correlation, we still used it here in LINEST:
   0.05   0.06   −0.01   −9.29
   weight height age   intercept

3. 2.87   3.09   3.39   3.69   3.80

Exercise 33.

There are more ways!

3. =ABS(A1 − Mean)

4. =IF(B1<(StDev/2), "", ">.5x")

5. =IF(B1<(StDev/2), "", IF(B1<StDev, ">.5x", ">1x"))

Exercise 34.

2. =VLOOKUP(52%,A1:E4,MATCH(92,A1:E1,1),TRUE)

3. =HLOOKUP(92,A1:E4,MATCH(52%,A1:A4,1),TRUE)

4. =INDEX(B2:E4,MATCH(52%,A2:A4,1),MATCH(92,B1:E1,1)) OR
   =INDEX(A1:E4,MATCH(52%,A1:A4,1),MATCH(92,A1:E1,1))

Exercise 35.

1. Five rows and four columns

Exercise 36.

4. Yes

A

Exercise 37.

2. =AVERAGE(IF(A1:A20>10,A1:A20))

3. =AVERAGE(A1:A20 - Mean)

4. =SUM(IF(D6:D18>3,1,0))

Exercise 38

2. Three arguments: initial As Integer, rate As Single, gens As Integer

3. It should return a Double

5. Double has a precision up to 15 digits and/or decimals, but can go much farther.

Exercise 39.

2. −10.25... and 9.75...

Exercise 40.

2. Use Data/Sort

4. Sort by the first column

7. Mean: 70 / Min: 65 / Max: 75

10. Select total table, then Format / Conditional Formatting, set Formula Is to =$D1="F", and set pattern to gray.

For additional exercises, use the interactive CD "Join the Excellers League," or "Excel for Scientists," available through www.mrexcel.com or www.amazon.com.

A

Index

IDX

IDX

IDX

IDX

IDX

IDX